From  to Son-Rise:

Lenten Sermons, 2017

Sermons for
Ash Wednesday Through Easter Sunday
Based on Readings From
the Revised Common Lectionary, Year A

Jack A. Wilder

Jack A. Wilder

Copyright © 2017 by Jack A. Wilder, Jr.

All rights reserved.

ISBN-10: 1547248025

ISBN-13:978-1547248025

Unless otherwise noted, scripture quotations are from the New Revised Standard Version Bible, copyright © 1989 the Division of Christian Education of the National Council of the Churches of Christ in the United States of America. Used by permission. All rights reserved.

Jack A. Wilder

DEDICATION

This volume is dedicated to my daughter, Ayla, who both reads and thinks profusely, and sometimes thinks deep thoughts about God.

ACKNOWLEDGMENTS

First I want to acknowledge my wife Leslie, my fellow proclaimer of the Good News of God in a crazy world, and, by a strange coincidence, the current pastor of Good Shepherd Lutheran Church, where my Lutheran journey, and the road that led me to where I am now, really began many years ago.

Second, I want to acknowledge those people who have listened to my sermons. They have given me feedback and encouraged me to publish my sermons. Most importantly, they have had the wisdom to let me be myself as I continue on my own journey as a pastor helping others to be themselves as they continue on their own journeys.

CONTENTS

Dedication	3
Acknowledgments	4
Forward	7
Ash Wednesday: Into the Tunnel of Lent	9
First Sunday in Lent: Into the Wilderness	14
First Midweek in Lent: All That Stuff	21
Second Sunday in Lent: Nicodemus	25
Second Midweek in Lent: Is That All Abraham Can Do?	31
Third Sunday in Lent: The Samaritan Woman	36
Third Midweek in Lent: God Is Like a Precocious Preschooler	42
Fourth Sunday in Lent: The Man Who Can See	46
Fourth Midweek in Lent: Shadows of Death, Children of Light	53
Fifth Sunday in Lent: Lazarus	58
Fifth Midweek in Lent: Flesh and Spirit and...	65
Sunday of the Passion/Palm Sunday: Amid the Hosannas and the Palms	70
Maundy Thursday: This Night Is Different	75
Good Friday: Cross, *Kairos,* New Creation	79
Easter Sunrise: Among the Graves	84

Easter Sunday: Son Rise 88

About the Author 94

FORWARD

Nicodemus, the Samaritan woman, the man blind from birth, Lazarus. These are the characters of the Lenten Gospel readings in Year A of the Revised Common Lectionary. These are characters that Jesus interacts with in very significant ways. In the stories of these characters, lives are influenced, lives are changed, and lives are made new by what Jesus says or by what he does to them and for them. But these stories are actually about something above and beyond the story of what happens with each character that meets Jesus.

In John chapter 3 we see that what Jesus said to Nicodemus had far greater importance and went far beyond being just a story about Jesus instructing a Pharisee about what it takes for one to see the Kingdom by "being born from above."

The story in the Gospel according to John is a story about the infinite compassion of the infinite God who both created the *cosmos* and is the embodiment of *agape* love. This infinite God loves the whole God-created *cosmos* with the *agape* love that truly *is* God. This infinite God, who is the embodiment of *agape* love, sends God's only Son, who himself is the embodiment of God, in order to live and die and live again for the sake of the whole world - for the sake of the entire *cosmos*. That *cosmos*, in the New Testament Greek of the Gospel of John, is the entirety of *everything* that is, the entirety of everything that ever was, and the entirety of everything that ever will be. Including all of humanity.

It is this cosmos-spanning, time-defying *agape* of God that Jesus himself embodies, lives, breathes, and acts upon for the sake of Nicodemus, the Samaritan woman, the blind man, Lazarus, and for every one of us today, now, wherever we are, whoever we are.

This *agape* is life-changing. It is a force for complete renewal. Life-giving, it is God's force for new creation, and as such, it is a force for turning around, renewing, and recreating entire congregations as much as individuals.

The sermons in this book are based on sermons that were delivered to a congregation struggling with renewal and with all the challenges that come with congregational renewal, including, but not limited to the search for a new identity and a new mission in a changing demographic. Among those challenges are critical decisions that have to be made, not least of which is the decision to intentionally embrace the empty tomb with the constructive changes that it brings, or to intentionally maintain the status quo as if the stone had never been rolled form the entrance to the tomb. Hopefully, these homilies have helped the congregation and individuals to move forward in their journey towards new life.

Lastly, for those who are curious about traditions regarding Nicodemus and the woman at the well, Jewish tradition regarding Nicodemus (a.k.a. Buni ben Gorion, Nakdimon) may be found in Josephus, *The Jewish War*, as well as *Tractate Ta'anit* in the *Babylonian Talmud* and several rabbinic works: the *Lamentations Rabbah*, the *Ecclesiastes Rabbah*, and the *Avot of Rabbi Natan*. The Jewish Virtual Library online also provides some information and provides references to ancient Jewish sources. Eastern Orthodox tradition contains material on St. Nicodemus as well as St. Photini/Photina, the woman at the well, "equal to the Apostles," who carries her witness of meeting Christ at the well to Rome where she is martyred.

Peace be with you!

Pr. J. Wilder
Easter, 2017

ASH WEDNESDAY

Into the Tunnel of Lent

Matthew 6:1-6, 16-21

Too many years ago, when I was taking my summer Greek class in seminary, our professor, we may call him "Charlie," greeted the class one morning about halfway through the course and told us that we were about to enter a long, dark tunnel. Our class was going to get harder. It was going to get more intense, and it was even going to become a little strange. (As if summer intensive Greek wasn't strange enough or intense enough for some of us.) A tremendous collective moan went up from the class. Understand that we had to sit in Greek class for six hours a day, five days a week. And we had more homework than you can shake a fist at. There were people who thought that class was hard enough already. *How* could it possibly get harder? *How* could it possibly get more intense?

But our professor told us not to despair, because, he said, that halfway through the week we would start to see the light at the end of the tunnel, and that at the end of the week we would emerge into the sunlight once again, with the end of summer Greek finally visible on the horizon. And he was right. But it was a very hard week for all of us, and that week some of us realized that we were growing in ways we did not expect when we began dreaming in conversational New Testament Greek. And *that*, I have to admit, was pretty strange.

Tonight we are entering into what must be the darkest, most intense, and strangest time of the Church year.

We begin the season of Lent with the decidedly strange practice of smearing ashes on our foreheads. As we do this, we start out on a Lenten journey that leads us step-by-slow step through a long, dark tunnel to a cross and a death and a tomb, and we know this even as we set out on the journey.

On this journey we are mindful of our human, weak, mortal nature. We acknowledge our absolute dependence on the grace of God. And we confess our absolute need for the faithfulness of Christ Jesus, the faithfulness of the one who was crucified, the faithfulness of the one who justifies us faithless humans upon his cross.

We need this reassurance of the faithfulness of Christ because the journey only seems to get darker as we venture deeper into the wilderness of Lent, while the Cross, with its pain, loneliness, death and tomb comes ever closer with each step.

And we do this, we undertake this journey into darkness *intentionally*, we Lutherans. This is something that we have in common with Roman Catholics and Anglicans and Presbyterians, and others, our brothers and sisters in the faith. But we Lutherans enter into Lent as if we are gluttons for punishment, which only gives credence to the joke that Lutherans only feel good when they feel guilty.

Perhaps this is why Lent is one of the most compelling times of the year for us.

Lent has traditionally been a penitential season. Traditionally, Lent has been a time for us to intentionally take stock of our sin, both our Big Sin and our little sins, and repent. But if we have paid attention to our Lutheran roots we know that we are called to repent on a daily basis. That is because, as sinful people, we cannot help but sin on a daily basis. That is why we need to be reminded of our baptism, our need for forgiveness, and our need for God's grace on a daily basis, as Martin Luther taught.

But that does not mean Lent is a time for us to wallow in the awareness of our sinful nature. To do that would not only be rather strange, an obsession on sin, but it would be toxic because it would be to give in to despair, to perpetually dwell in the long, dark tunnel of Lent, and not to see the light at the end of the tunnel.

Lent is a time to *grow* and *move forward* in our journey. We do this by using Lent as a time to intentionally pause, re-focus, reflect, discern, listen, learn, recommit, and grow. Our setting aside time for mid-week Lenten services is one way to help us do that in a healthy way, not by beating ourselves up because we have all sinned and fallen short of the glory of God. That's not what the ashes of Ash Wednesday are about. But by looking for the Jesus who has compassion for the sinner. And that is what the ashes are about.

The ashes on our foreheads remind us that we are in extreme need of the deep forgiving and healing compassion of Christ. This is compassion for the outcast. It is compassion for the fallen and the rejected. It is compassion for the weak. Compassion for those who have failed, those who are in despair, those who have given up, and those who need to be lifted to new life. They are the people whom Jesus seeks out and invites to be the first to enter into the Kingdom of God. Not those who feel that they are already righteous in their own right and of their own accord (recall the attitudes of the Pharisees), and feel that they do not need a new life. But it is compassion for those who live their lives sitting in despair on a heap of ashes (recall Job, who sat on his ash heap), those who dwell in darkness (recall Isaiah), those who have lost their way in the long, dark tunnel that their life has become, and those who await, perhaps without even realizing that they need it, the redeeming light of Christ.

Tonight, as we begin our Lenten journey in the midst of ashes (admit it, it does seem a strange way to enter into Lent), we do not set out to be like the hypocrites, those stage-actors who pretend to be something other than what they really are, as the original meaning of the word went. Jesus instructs us not to be like those who only pretend to be righteous, but are in reality anything but righteous. The direct connection to Christ's words about storing up treasures for oneself on earth more than a little implies that those who intentionally disfigure themselves are doing so because they seek some sort of gain and profit in this world.

Would that be a financial gain? Maybe someone, somewhere, will seek financial gain through hypocrisy, but more likely the hypocrites seek to gain:

Attention. Influence. Ego gratification. Praise for an insincere morality. The triumph of false ethics. Self-justification before God. The delusion of glory, The fulfillment of vindictive wishes against their neighbors. The parading of a false and shallow righteousness. And plain old narcissism. (I think that what I call the American Religious Industrial Complex is all about promoting these kinds of things as a false spirituality.)

But in the end, all of that stuff is defined by one simple word: "Sin," with a capital "S." And all of that stuff is foolishness in the real Old Testament sense of the word. It is foolishness because it blindly seeks petty, personal, and even destructive gain in a world that deeply and dramatically needs the gift of healing, forgiving, and freeing compassion that only the Son of God can give.

So, the bottom line is that we are reminded by the ashes tonight that we face a certain type of darkness as we begin Lent. It is a human darkness. In that darkness we face our deep need for the light for Christ's compassion. Charlie's "long, dark tunnel," perhaps.

There is something compelling about it all, this business about darkness and death and coming closer to the cross, because there is a compelling, unending, growing light framing the darkness.

That light framing the darkness is that act of Jesus going to die on a cross. Here is a singular eschatological act of salvation for the entirety of humanity, past, present, and future. It is an act Jesus performs so that we who are only mere mortals, with all our deep darkness, may, after everything, rise up to a new light and become a part of God's new creation. Lent may be dark, intense, and strange, as seasons of the church year go, but Lent at its bottom line is about hope.

There is already a light shining beyond the end of the long, dark tunnel of Lent. It is slowly but steadily growing, inch by inch, day by day, just the other side of the cross, and at the darkest moment, when the time is just right, the light rises eternal to banish the darkness forever.

This journey that leads to the cross continues and goes far beyond the cross. It trudges up to the point of death at the cross - there but for the grace of God we go - and then, at the cross, when it seems that we are standing on the edge of eternal darkness, we are taken by the hand by the crucified Lord. And while we are in his hands we find that our Lenten journey ultimately plunges us straight through death itself so that we may soar beyond into endless new life high among all the saints in the ever shining Kingdom of God.

Peace be with you!

FIRST SUNDAY IN LENT

Into the Wilderness

Matthew 4:1-11

"Then the devil left him, and suddenly angels came and waited on him." (Matthew 4:11.)

I always thought that was a strange way for Matthew to end the story of the temptation of Jesus. This was especially so whenever I heard the text read in some other versions of the Bible where it says that these messengers of God "ministered" to Jesus. What? What the heck is that supposed to mean? Think about it. What was this generic "ministering" that was going on? And what sort of meaning is this supposed to have for us? It never made sense to me as a teenager and young adult, and for years I could never find any one person (or any one commentary) who could give me a straight or believable answer.

The text today comes from the New Revised Standard Version where it says in Matthew 4:11 that angels came and "waited on" Jesus. That's a little bit better, but not much. At least it doesn't say that generic angels popped in out of nowhere and did some sort of generic, undefined, mysterious but meaningless-to-the-reader "ministry" with/to/or for Jesus. It's still very odd, but I understand why the NRSV renders Matthew's words that way. Matthew uses a word for the angels' activity that literal means "waiting on tables."

"What!" we exclaim. "Waiting on tables for Jesus! In the wilderness! After forty days of fasting and temptation! That's just silly!" And I guess the image it conjures up for the modern reader *is* silly. Do the angels appear with an outdoor cafe, waiters, little round tables and fat free French Vanilla latte? Perhaps, in the Monty Python version of the Gospel. Well, Matthew did use the same word that we find in the Book of Acts where the Apostles chose deacons whose initial purpose was to wait on tables and feed the hungry.

But still, neither of those ways of reading Matthew really works for us because neither of those ways makes sense to us. But there is a third way of reading and understanding what Matthew was saying, and Matthew did mean to be understood. The word Matthew uses, which many translators have rendered as "ministered to" or "waited on" also means "to serve," and not just in the sense that one is waiting on tables and feeding people. The deacons of Acts were to do much more than just serve as "waiters." Remember the deacon Stephen? His primary role in Acts was not to be a waiter but to serve Christ and carry out his will as a witness, ultimately proclaiming the gospel. *Now* that last line in the reading makes better sense. This is not about angels serving as waiters for a hungry Jesus. This is about serving as in *carrying out a person's will and doing those things that someone wants done.*

Today we approach Matthew not from the beginning of the story, but from the end. At the end of the story we find Jesus, hungry, dirty, haggard, and ragged, after forty days in a deserted location in the Judean countryside. He has been exposed to the elements, fasting, and apparently fighting his own, private battle against an unseen and wicked bad adversary. And after going through that ordeal, the servants of God suddenly come to him, accept him as their Lord and master, and begin to serve him in some way that his will is done. And yes, someone may still say, without much thought, "Well, yes, Jesus was hungry, so they served him by feeding him!" But I don't believe Matthew meant the text to be understood in such a shallow way. Remember that deacons (and Matthew's choice of words makes it clear that the "angels" here are serving as "deacons") did (and still do!) so much more than "wait on tables."

At the end of the story we are not only reminded of the Lord's Prayer again, where we pray, "Your will be done, on earth as in heaven," but in that last line from the story we see the final victory scene in which Jesus has defeated evil and the false lords that seek to rule this world. This is a scene that foreshadows the final victory of Christ the King who brings in the Kingdom of God, sets the world to rights, and celebrates with an eschatological feast. We are reminded by Matthew 4:11 of the vision of Isaiah in which all the nations of the world are drawn to the mountain of God and join in a great feast.

And this is just the end of Matthew's temptation story; we haven't even got to the beginning yet. The end is a good place to begin, however, because we can go back and read the story again with this ending in mind. When we do, then the story suddenly makes a lot more sense and takes on a lot more meaning for us.

Back in the day, when Jesus went alone into the wilderness, it was common practice for Jewish men to set out alone into the countryside, away from towns and human presence, in order to go through a spiritual experience for forty days. This was something they did when they were beginning a new spiritual calling, or committing themselves to a spiritual ministry or journey. They did this to strengthen themselves spiritually and to cleanse themselves spiritually for the mission ahead of them. Anyone could have done this back then. You could have done it. But just because someone went into the wilderness and subjected themselves to spiritual trials and temptations doesn't make that person the Son of God. But there is something different about this one person, Jesus, and there is something different about his wilderness experience, and Matthew wants his readers to know this.

Matthew begins the story with words that brought to mind epic stories for those who listened to the Gospel when it was new. Jesus was "led up by the Spirit into the wilderness," and to say that in his own words, Matthew borrowed the wording of epic stories about heroes who took to the wine dark sea and set sail, with hazards and perils ahead of them, monsters and adversaries to fight, discoveries to be made, and victory awaiting them. Matthew has Jesus setting sail with the wind of the Spirit at his back, but his vast, empty sea is a barren, deserted wilderness, and the monster he had to face, and his trials and temptations are of a different type than those found in the epic stories of the day.

Jesus goes into the wilderness for the purpose of facing the evil one, Mr. Diablo, otherwise known as the devil.

Forty days come and go. Jesus has been undergoing a fast, basically a starvation diet with water, and he just might be involved in the same type of prayer that I mentioned last week when I talked about the vision of Peter, James, and John on the Mount of the Transfiguration, that type of Jewish meditation practiced by people who secluded themselves in isolated places, the type of prayer in which one expects to receive a spiritual vision. If so, then boy, did he get it.

After forty days diablo appears, as in a spiritual vision, confident, self-assured, tricky, hiding behind a false front of sincerity and friendliness. Matthew's name for the devil is *diabolos.* It means the "Diabolical One," literally, the one who throws an obstacle (even himself!) across your path to make you stumble, stop you, and cause you to become lost. He is the "Evil One." And he has a simple, seemingly harmless agenda. The Evil One wants Jesus to prove himself. That's the meaning of the word for "tempting" that Matthew uses. Jesus is called upon to prove he is the Son of God, and this is evident from the way the Evil One talks to him:

"If you are the Son of God, command these stones to become loaves of bread." (Matthew 4:3.)

What he's saying is: "Prove to me you are the Son of God. I'll even make it easy for you to do this! You're so hungry now, you could eat a cart load of bread! It's understandable, and I sympathize with you. I feel your pain, I truly do! So, command these stones to become loaves of bread, and it will all be OK. No one will find fault with you if you feed yourself!" But if Jesus did that, then the Evil One would prove that he was self-serving, feeding himself with the food meant to feed a multitude.

And Jesus refuses. One does not live by bread alone, but by every word that comes from God. Life is not to be guided by our instinctive wants and needs with the promise of quick and easy gratification. Life is to be guided by the will of God, and sometimes the path that the will of God leads us down is anything but quick and easy.

Failure! No matter. The Evil One decides to try again. In the wilderness vision the Evil One takes Jesus to the highest point of the monumental temple in Jerusalem. The entire Jewish nation, Jews across the Roman world, looked to the city of God, Jerusalem, and the Temple, the "House of God," for signs of God's coming Kingdom and for indications of God's will being enacted in the world. Pharisees even taught that when the Messiah finally came, he would descend from heaven directly above Jerusalem and come straight to the Temple. There, on holy ground, at the focal point of the faith and the expectations of Jews everywhere, the Evil One again calls on Jesus to prove himself:

"If you are the Son of God, then throw yourself off into the empty heights and let yourself fall, because it is written that God will command angels to lift you up so that you are not to be hurt. Do you not see what you can do! Everyone will accept you as the Messiah! Do you not want this?" (Matthew 4:6, my paraphrase.)

The Evil One wants Jesus to put on a miracle show, the type of miracle show that many had already said they would like to see, the kind of thing that would prove to many that someone, in this case Jesus, is the Messiah. And if the Evil One succeeds, then he may have demonstrated that Jesus is the Son of God, but he will also have demonstrated that he has power over the Son of God, that he can literally make the Son of God jump. Then the Evil One's will, and not God's will, would be done, even on holy ground.

Once again, Jesus refuses. This time the refusal is blunt and direct: "Again it is written: 'Do not put the Lord your God to the test.'" (Matthew 4:7.)

Well, that didn't work. Let's try something new and different! The Evil One takes Jesus up to a high mountain. Recall the Mount of the Transfiguration? It may be the same mountain in this scene. One can see far and wide here, and the Evil One then calls on Jesus, not to prove himself, but to simply fall down and worship him, and in return he would give Jesus the kingdoms of the world, making Jesus the new Caesar. This was actually the hope of the Pharisees, that the Messiah would rule the world as a new and better Caesar. And hasn't this also been the hope of many religious people since then? Now Jesus would have the chance to prove to many that he really was the Messiah! The kind of Messiah they expected, the kind of Messiah acceptable to the world: the kind of Messiah who would worship the Evil One.

And Jesus once again refuses, but this time his refusal is aggressive and commanding. This time Jesus names the Evil One as Satan, the Adversary: "Get lost, Satan! Because it has been written, worship the Lord your God, and serve only him!" (Matthew 4:10, my paraphrase.)

And then, without much ado, not even a "So long, see you later," the Evil One went away. The vision of temptation then ends, and we return to the place where we began, the end of the story, where the servants of God arrive in the aftermath of the confrontation and serve Jesus, so that his will is done. And probably the end scene with the angels was also a part of the whole spiritual vision in the wilderness, but even so, it has meaning, or Matthew would not have included it in the story.

The bottom line is that in the end, the will of Jesus will be carried out, and the will of Jesus is that the will of God be done, right here on earth, as it is in heaven. The will of God is *not* that Jesus, the Son of God, should be a self-serving Messiah who feeds himself first while ignoring a starving humanity, but that he should be one who feeds the vast multitude who were awaiting the true Bread of Life.

The will of God is *not* that Jesus, the Messiah, should reduce the mighty acts of God to a cheap and shallow miracle show to wow the masses, but that the Messiah should be raised up higher than the temple for another purpose altogether, rising on a cross to redeem and lift high the entire fallen world with him.

The will of God is *not* that Jesus, the Savior of the World, should become a new and better Caesar, ruling in the Kingdom of the Evil One, but that Jesus should bring in God's Kingdom, the Kingdom that sets the world to rights and brings with it an entirely new creation.

And this Jesus, who defies having to prove himself, is the Jesus who brings the Kingdom near to *us*, frail and weak mortals one and all who live daily with trials and temptations and demands that we prove ourselves to an unsympathetic, legalistic, hostile, and uncaring world. This is the Jesus who forgives our sins. This is the Jesus who would die for us. This is the Son of God who brings us into the realm of God's infinite compassion.

This is why Jesus entered the wilderness, not for himself, because he has proved that he is not self-serving, *but for us*, that we and all the world may at last be included in the Kingdom of God.

Peace be with you!

Jack A. Wilder

FIRST MIDWEEK IN LENT

All That Stuff

Romans 5:12-19

Sin and death. Sin and more death! Sin, law, and death again! *More* sin, and transgression on top of that! These are the subjects of the first three verses of the Romans reading. Obviously, there's a lot of sin and death going on in the reading, a lot of sin and death on the minds of the people Paul wrote to, and a lot of sin and death that Paul feels compelled to address. Do we *really* want to get into a reading like this? I don't know. We might want to reconsider our Lenten observance, although our Lenten taco bar might make it all worth it.

The first three verses of the reading are, at first glance, so loaded with sin and death that they make Romans 5 seem like it must be the kind of reading that makes Lent what it has always traditionally been: a time of guilt, confession, penitence, and more guilt, feeling bad about ourselves because we are but weak mortals, faulty human beings who fall far short of the glory of God, or as Martin Luther said in one of his more creative moments, nothing but maggot fodder destined to die. (The specific quote about maggot fodder is found in Martin Luther, "A Sincere Admonition to All Christians to Guard Against Insurrection and Rebellion" (1522), Luther's Works, Vol. 45, p. 70. Luther was specifically speaking about himself in an attempt to repudiate the use of his name in identifying the church that had started as a result of his work.) "Maggot fodder." Really makes you want to observe Lent, doesn't it?

But Luther always points us back to the Apostle Paul, and let's not misunderstand Paul. Paul is not the Apostle of Gloom and Doom. He is not the poster child of the stereotyped Gotta-Feel-Bad-in-Order-to-Feel-Good Lutherans. Paul didn't even know what a Lutheran was. He is not an advocate of dwelling in guilt. To the contrary. Paul rails against death with clenched fists. He rejects guilt as a failed life style. He condemns sin as a self-destructive addiction. He has no interest in making us feel bad about ourselves. But he also has no fear in addressing the most brutal aspects of human existence, and he must do it in his own way.

Tonight we start our mid-week Lenten meditation with the Big Picture, as the Apostle Paul understood it, as a small group of Roman Christians either wanted or needed to hear it, and as he wrote it out in his own personal, sketchy, shorthand style.

This reading from Romans was one of the topics of conversation at our adult Bible study last Sunday. It made for some interesting conversation, partly because of the intensity of the reading, and partly because of the scope of the reading, because what Paul does is address the entirety of human existence, from the beginning with its proverbial Adam, to the end with Christ.

It is a lot of territory to cover. Huge numbers of books have been written about that territory. Paul covers it all in just a few lines. How can he possibly do that? Does he not take the subject seriously? Has he not thought it through adequately? Does he not respect his readers?

To the contrary!

Paul was once a member of what we might call the Judean Religious Industrial Establishment - it was very similar to what I call the American Religious Industrial Establishment of today. Paul was once part of an organized religion that promoted and profited from making people suffer from guilt and obsess over sin and its consequence, death, while dangling remedies for sin and death before people, sometimes remedies unobtainable by the vast majority of poor and suffering humanity. And what is that if it is not intentional cruelty? A few people benefited from this, financially, and in other ways. For a while, Paul was one of those people. He understood the complexity of the system, and the complexity of the problem that the system was built to address and to exploit. And he knew that the whole thing had been made artificially and unnecessarily complicated, not by God, but by sinful people who presumed to offer fail-safe solutions to the fatal problem of sin.

That will surely be an over-simplification of religion at the time of Paul, but we face the same dilemma Paul faced in his letter to the Romans: presenting a topic vast in scope and depth, with a very limited time in which to address it tonight.

Paul didn't deal with all the endless debate and talk about the problem of sin and death and what to do about it. He wasn't going to waste time and energy with that kind of nonsense. He had something more important to do, and he was going to do it quickly and effectively. Paul took the whole big convoluted mess and brought it all down to its lowest common denominators: Adam and Christ.

Drawing from the Genesis stories, Paul tells us that human sin began with the first human, and since then death has ruled human existence. The Religious Industrial Complex would have said, "No sweat. We have ways to deal with that." Pharisees would have said, "OK, the solution to the whole thing is to obey the law and obey it with perfection." Priests would have said, "The real solution to the problem is Temple worship and sacrifices - as much as possible, regardless of the cost." Others would have had other solutions, such as fasting, living in isolation in the desert, self-sacrifice, and other faulty human works.

But Paul did not do that. Paul took an approach that no one had ever taken before. First he took everything that the Religious Industrial Complex had to offer and he tossed it out the window. Be gone, Processed Religion! Then he took Adam and he said, "You see this guy in Genesis, Adam, back at the beginning? Look at him. All of sin came into the world through him, and along with it came death, and as a result, many died."

Then he pointed to Christ Jesus at the other end of the story. "You see that guy, Christ? He brought the free gift of the grace of God into this world, and because of the free gift, many will live."

And people will immediately want to object: "But Paul, what about the Religious Industrial Establishment? What about the Pharisees?

The priests? What about our diet of artificially Processed Religion? What about all that *stuff*? Surely, *we have to have our stuff in order to be saved!*"

And Paul tells us to toss all that stuff out. All that stuff does not save us. All that stuff does is lead us into despair because it compels us to create our own failed salvation with our own mortal hands: Processed Religion. Toss all that stuff out, because just as one man's trespass led to condemnation for all, so one man's act of righteousness leads to justification and life for all. The many who were made sinners will be made righteous by the one man's obedience. Here we are reminded that Paul talks in Philippians 2:8 of Jesus as the one who was obedient unto death on a cross, and that was for *our* sake, *our* welfare, *our* healing, *our* justification, *our* relationship with God, and *our* place in the Kingdom.

And there we have it: the Good News of Christ in Paul. And this is the Good News of Lent: that though there is sin and death in this world, there is also no condemnation, because Christ Jesus brings to us many sinners the free gift of God's righteousness. This righteousness of God rejects our guilt, condemns our self-destructive sin, addresses the most brutal aspects of human existence, and totally and completely remakes us as new creations who live in the image of God. Makes you want to observe Lent, doesn't it?

Peace be with you!

SECOND SUNDAY IN LENT

Nicodemus

John 3:1-17

Let's start with a brief history lesson, because history is fun!

When we read Jewish history, we find the story of a young man whose name was Buni the son of Gorion. Buni came from a long line of Pharisees. His father, his grandfather, and great grandfather were all Pharisees. So when he got his education, Buni went to one of the schools of the Pharisees, the best school in Jerusalem, one of the two schools that met in the Temple itself. He was brilliant. He was a genius. He excelled in his studies. He became a Pharisee, a teacher of Israel with pride. He was a man of integrity, and he was respected even by his enemies, the priests, and by other Pharisees who were envious of him.

While still relatively young he came to sit on the highest court in the Jewish world, the Great Sanhedrin in Jerusalem, and he came hold a political office that today we would call the "mayor of Jerusalem." And if that was not enough, he became exceedingly wealthy. By the time he was middle-aged, he was living the Pharisees' dream. Many years later, when he was an old man and his sons had grown to become Pharisees, the Roman general Titus laid siege to Jerusalem. Buni and his family had fled the supposed safety of the city before the Romans came, just as many Christians had fled. Then he and his sons tried to negotiate with Titus to bring about a peaceful resolution to the conflict. However that negotiation played out, Buni failed, and the rest is a great tragedy for Jerusalem.

Not long afterwards, Titus would go on to become Caesar. Buni, the son of Gorion, would also become known by a very different name in history. While he was still the "mayor of Jerusalem," still young, self-assured, and daring, he made a deal with Pontius Pilate. A bet, really, against the odds, but on behalf of the people of the city so that they would have water during a drought. And he succeeded, against the odds. This made him very popular with the people of the city, who began to think of him as a miracle worker and started to call him by an Aramaic name that more or less means something like, "He On Whom the Sun Shines" (*Babylonian Talmud*, tractate Ta'anit, folio 20a), or, if you like, "That Lucky Guy." [*Nak-di-mon*, for those of you who keep track of Aramaic names.]

But Greek-speaking Jews in the city didn't like Aramaic names. They didn't like the way Aramaic sounds. They thought it was an ugly language, not like Greek. So, they changed Buni's nickname to something that at least sounded Greek, and could be said to have some meaning in Greek that might be related to his victory over Pontius Pilate on behalf of the people. They called him *Nicodemus*.

One night in Jerusalem, Nicodemus came to see Jesus. Much has happened before this. Jesus has overthrown the tables of the money changers and forcefully driven them out of the temple, along with the animals being sold for sacrifice. He has confronted the priests and not backed down. The priests are even afraid of him, and the high priest, Joseph Caiaphas, has decided Jesus must die. Many people of the city and the Galilean pilgrims hail him as Messiah.

By now the three houses of the Great Sanhedrin are talking about Jesus. The House of the Chief Priests, the Sadducees, led by Caiaphas, wants to kill him if possible, but *how*? The House of the Elders, all Pharisees, has long been opposed to the House of the Chief Priests. They are beginning to favor Jesus, who defies the priests and claims he can rebuild the temple in three days. The membership of the House of the Scribes is divided between Pharisees and priests, but it leans towards the House of the Chief Priests. Conspiracy, intrigue, scandal, and politics, the hallmarks of a deeply broken humanity and its toxic religion, are in the air that night as Nicodemus and whoever escorted him went through dark narrow streets to find the house where Jesus stayed.

The mayor of Jerusalem must be careful. He must be discrete. He cannot be seen openly, by day, associating with Jesus. The political risk is too great. But he has to know. Quite possibly he is the leader of the House of the Elders and their spokesman. When he finds Jesus he speaks not only for himself, but for the others as well:

"*We* know that you are a teacher who has come from God, because *no one* can do the signs that you do apart from God." (John 3:2, my paraphrase.)

What is Nicodemus looking for, exactly? Is he validating Jesus? Does he expect Jesus to rise up and rule Israel as the expected Messiah in the militaristic and political manner expected by the Pharisees? John doesn't spell it out. We have only the condensed Reader's Digest version of a conversation that is found nowhere else in the Gospels. John gives us only the most important statements, the next statement coming from Jesus:

"This is true: No one can see the Kingdom of God without being born from above." (John 3:3, my paraphrase.)

More questions arise. Is Jesus validating Nicodemus? Is he saying, "You have seen the Kingdom of God! You have been born from above!" It's as if some intermediate statements are missing; the part of me that is a historian, not to mention the part of me that is a theologian, gripes and grumbles about getting the Reader's Digest version. But John has just given us two very important points that John wants every disciple to have so that they may believe:

First: Jesus has come from God. Second: Only those who are "born from above" may see the Kingdom of God.

But that second statement leads to a valid common sense question that could be asked by anyone: "How can anyone be born after being old?" (John 3:4, my translation of the Greek text.)

This is where people make the assumption that Nicodemus must have been an old man when he talked with Jesus, but really this is not necessarily so. What we see in the text is the type of questioning that Pharisees and rabbis commonly used when discussing matters pertaining to God. It's the same type of question and answer dialogue that teachers used when teaching their disciples. The observant Lutherans who remember their confirmation classes from many years ago will recognize this interaction between Nicodemus and Jesus as a catechism.

Another way to state Nicodemus' question is, "You say one must be born from above to see the Kingdom? Very well, what about an old man?" That is a way to ask how that person has any hope of seeing the Kingdom. What Nicodemus is really saying is, "What about any person of any age who has already been born of this world? How is that person to be born from above, now, today?"

This is the million dollar question, isn't it? *"What must I do to be saved? What must I say? What hoops must I jump through?"* The Religious Industrial Establishment will always be happy to tell you exactly what you must do to be saved. Pharisees and priests had all kinds of ways for you to influence God and buy your salvation: obey these laws, make these sacrifices.

Today the hawkers of popular American Processed Religion do much the same thing: say this prayer, do these things, make this decision, find Jesus (*as if he were the one who was lost*!), do something that you can later boast and brag about before the audience of Processed Religion customers and call it a "testimony!"

Nicodemus is asking what must be done. He simply wants Jesus to clarify his theology: "You say one must be born from above. How is this done? Must I jump through hoops? Must I go through some sort of mystery rites? What must be done by the one who seeks to see the Kingdom?" And the answer is nothing so spectacular as Nicodemus imagines, but it is no less miraculous:

One enters the Kingdom by being born of water and the Spirit. And Jesus says the Spirit will do what it wants. It will go where it wants. It moves as freely as the wind, meaning, like it or not, that just *anyone* can be born of the Spirit. Just *anyone*, anyone like...

The poor. The lame. The deaf. The mute. The sick. The hungry. The homeless. The tax collectors. The sinners. The outcasts. The rejected. The snubbed. The bullied. The weak. The old. All of those people that Jesus has had and still has compassion for, even Pharisees like Nicodemus who believe that Jesus has come from

God.

Well, this is big. This is really **BIG**. This is probably much more than Nicodemus and those he spoke for had suspected. This is much more than the petty-but-lethal conspiracy, intrigue, scandal, and politics that had occupied Pharisees and priests for so many years. This is much more than Caiaphas and the priests saw in their worst nightmares. This blows away all Processed Religion. This puts the Religious Industrial Establishment out of business. This is much more than any of them had ever dreamed, and if *this* is what the Kingdom of God is really like, if the Spirit is truly unbound and goes just *anywhere*, and if just *anyone* can enter the Kingdom...then the consequences for this world and for everyone who has ever lived have got to be beyond belief.

"How can these things be?" Nicodemus asks. (John 3:10.) He seems to be stunned by what he has heard. Jesus gives him the bottom line: These things can be "For God so loved the world that he gave his only Son, so that everyone who believes in him may not perish but may have eternal life." (John 3:16.)

And this is so because, "Indeed, God did not send the Son into the world to condemn the world, but in order that the world might be saved through him." (John 3:17.)

Nicodemus probably went away that night thinking that, yes, he and the others were right about Jesus. Jesus has indeed come from God. Nicodemus probably went away with both validation and hope: he has seen the Kingdom of God in what Jesus was doing, so he must be born from above. And if that is true, then he is already a part of the eternal Kingdom. But what a Kingdom it must be, in which *just anyone* can enter and freely live a new life within the bounds of God's compassion!

Meanwhile, what of us? We hear the Good News because of the Holy Spirit, freely sent by Jesus, the Son. This is the Spirit that is freely working in our lives, and often working upstream, moving against the current of our lives. And this Spirit can go to anyone it wants without restriction and without qualification. The Spirit will bring just anyone it wants to faith and trust in Jesus, usually people we might least expect. And it will bring anyone it wants to see the Kingdom that Jesus brings near to all of us every day through his death and rising.

That Kingdom that Jesus brings near every day is a Kingdom of God's boundless compassion for a world in deep brokenness. Jesus brings that Kingdom near to all of us. The Spirit compels us to enter the Kingdom on sheer faith alone (*passive trust!*), and we are called to trust as we go, to trust that God loves the whole of creation, to trust that God loves us, and to trust God wholly and completely.

Because of Jesus who died on the cross for us, God will not chastise us for deeds done before we have been reborn children of God. The past will be forgiven and forgotten. The future will lie before us as a clean slate.

No matter what has happened to us in life, no matter what we have done, no matter where we have been or what we have thought or said or believed before, the compassion of God is enfolding us and awaiting us to trust.

As we continue in our Lenten journey let us trust Christ to make our life new again as reborn children of God, people born from above as new creations in the image of the God who makes all things new.

Peace be with you!

SECOND MIDWEEK IN LENT

Is That All Abraham Can Do?

Romans 4:1-5

"What should we say was gained by Abraham?" (Romans 4:1a, my paraphrase.)

I don't know, Paul. What are we to say?

Consider Abraham. He was a homeless nomad, a vagabond, a wandering Aramean. He left his wealthy father's fine home in Mesopotamia and took off to follow this weird, new, unheard-of, invisible God of the desert to...who knows where? He didn't know where he was going. He just listened to a voice that came out of nowhere, a voice in his head, perhaps, a voice that urged him onward, that seemed to be leading him to...nowhere.

One has to wonder if Abraham was entirely sane in order for him to do that. Today, if people tell us they hear voices out of nowhere, we'd say they need professional psychiatric help. In my imagination, in the great historical novel I'm going to write some day, Abraham was more than a little bit off his rocker. And maybe he was, who knows? But God works by different rules than we imagine, and tends to pick people who are not quite right to do great things: people like Moses, David, Paul...

This invisible God, whom Abraham could not see, but could hear, made a promise to him. God wasn't just leading Abraham around for the fun of it. Oh, no. There was a method to God's madness, if wandering about homeless in the Middle Eastern wilderness be madness. At one point during Abraham's wandering God led Abraham out under the stars at night and made an enormous promise to him about a vast future. God told Abraham that he would become the father of a nation, a multitude of people, and that his people would inherit the earth. And last, but not least, this invisible God took the initiative and made a covenant with Abraham, "cut a covenant," was the actual phrase they used then. And this crazy God, who was leading Abraham on a crazy journey, actually assumed the role of the one who was responsible and accountable to Abraham. The cutting of this covenant demonstrated that *God* was willing to pay the cost for keeping the covenant, despite the prevailing wisdom at the time which said it should have been the other way around. *People* cut covenants with gods. *Mortal human beings* made promises to gods. *People* paid the cost of keeping those promises, too, and the cost was often paid in blood and with a life given as a sacrifice. Who is this backwards God? Abraham, can you not even follow a divinity that makes sense? Really, what divine being is going to offer himself as a sacrifice in order to keep the covenant? Is your God as mad as you are? Abraham, you are daft! You are a fool!

Well, Paul, what are we to say was gained by Abraham?

Paul likes to begin his arguments by stating rhetorical questions like that. Up to this point, in Romans chapter three, Paul has been talking about covenant justice and justification, law and faith. I really think that part of chapter three should be tacked onto the lectionary reading here for that reason, because, together with tonight's reading, it forms one long thought from a man who was notorious for long thoughts.

Tonight Paul's long thought leads us to Abraham, the wandering Aramean. What are we to say was gained by this vagabond? God made a promise to him. OK. So what did our intrepid nomad gain? Was Abraham justified, made right with God, by his weak, frail works, his mortal deeds, his fallible actions? If so, then he did have something to brag about.

But not before God!

Paul has appealed to the very foundational moment of the Hebrew people by referring to Abraham and the covenant with its incredible promise. Now he appeals directly to the Hebrew Bible. What does the scripture say? What is written?

"Abraham believed God, and it was reckoned to him as righteousness." (Romans 4:3b.)

Another way to put it is that Abraham *passively trusted* God, and God *actively worked out the math of righteousness* in his favor, indicating that Abraham was in the right. God made a great promise to Abraham, cut a covenant, and all Abraham did, and all Abraham had to do, was *trust* this strange God of the covenant. All that was required was that he *passively trust* the God who indicated by cutting the covenant that God would do the unthinkable: *sacrifice himself in order to keep the covenant.*

But *trust*? Is that all Abraham can do? He has been on a lifetime journey, following God year after year, even facing mortal danger once in a while. Can he not do *more* than just *trust*? Surely he must, right? To do otherwise offends our modern American values of self-reliance and independence, not to mention that it is offensive to the American Religious Industrial Establishment. After all, what is trust if it is not lazy? Dependent? Passive? Surely Abraham must have done or is about to do the "right thing" in order to keep the covenant! Our modern church population, fed on a diet of artificial Processed Religion, would say that Abraham would have had to do The Thing that would make him right with his God of the covenant. American cheap pop religion urges us to look for a decision, a prayer, a chest beating confession, a sacrifice, a vow, an attitude, a good deed done well to prove that Abraham was right with God.

Paul, however, disagrees with us. The God of the covenant is the one who is responsible, under the covenant, for making things right between humanity and God. To try to force it the other way around, to become legalistic, to become self-righteous, was to become faithless. So Paul tells us,

> "For the promise that he would inherit the world did not come to Abraham or to his descendants through the law..." (Romans 4:13a.)

The implication, as Paul spells it out, is just plain common sense and it is powerful.

"If it is the adherents of the law who are to be the heirs, faith is null and the promise is void. Because the law brings wrath..." (Romans 4:14-15a.)

The bottom line, as we consider Abraham, is that we will not inherit God's promise, a vast future, the Kingdom of God and all that comes with it, by being obedient little soldiers for God. The call to serve as Christ served is not a call to self-salvation through works of our own doing, but it is a call to lose ourselves as we serve others, and to let God act through Christ on the cross to do all the saving that needs to be done.

That whole self-salvation rat race, something that is prevalent in our modern do-it-yourself American religion, is something that begins with the story in Genesis 3, where a serpent gives the first humans the first ever dose of Processed Religion by telling them that not only will they not die, but that they can also become like God if they choose to eat from the tree of knowledge of good and evil, and the rest of the story goes downhill from there. From the beginning people have tried to become like God and save themselves.

The desire to have it all drives us, frail mortals that we are, wandering through life from one day to the next and not knowing where we are going, to do everything that we can possibly do so that we may make this world ours, have as much life as possible, and bring ourselves closer to God in the process, so that in some way we may construct some assurance of our salvation.

Perhaps it is our primal survival instinct. Perhaps it is fear-driven anxiety that compels us to chase after ultimate laws, and human hubris that deceives us into believing that our mortal hands may grasp the ultimate in order to bring us to our personal eternal salvation.

Perhaps it is all psychological; a narcissistic greed, a psychotic desire for power, a sociopathic need to win the game of life at everyone else's expense, the delusion that personal eternal glory is waiting for us just around the corner if we only obey, do the right thing, and make ourselves like God through our obedience to law.

Or, perhaps we should just keep it simple, and just call it our plain old sinful nature, that ultimate rebellious desire to be like God so that we may gain the world and more.

No wonder then, that the promise of God, the promise that Abraham would inherit the world, did not and will not come to Abraham, or to his descendants, or to any of us through the law, through the things we do or say or think or believe.

To go that route leads us on a journey into nothing but wrath, as Paul pointed out; that furious reordering of God that sets us back on the path we should have been on all along.

But to *passively trust*...to *believe*...to just rely on *simple faith and nothing more*, to be passive and turn it all over to the God who will sacrifice himself on a cross in order to keep the covenant, to trust in God's righteousness, God's goodness, God's will, and God's Son who embodies God on the cross, **that is the way** that we are called to go on our Lenten journey.

Peace be with you!

THIRD SUNDAY IN LENT

The Samaritan Woman

John 4:5-42

Today we have a very long Gospel reading and I'm only going to focus on a part of it so we can deal with the Samaritan woman. The reading brings us to Jacob's well at the Samaritan town of Sychar.

At the time of Jesus, the site of the well was a local legend almost 2000 years old. When Abraham needed to rest from following his invisible God, he camped at the site of that well and remained there for many years. Jacob also stayed there when he needed to rest from his journeys. Now Jesus needed to rest for a couple of days on his journey.

Did he plan this? Did he realize the significance of taking his rest at Jacob's well? Or was it all just coincidence?

As the story opens, we find Jesus in the position of Jacob and Abraham, like a new patriarch of a new Israel, whose mere presence has special significance. God has been to this place on the map before. Now that Jesus has arrived, God has returned to an old and familiar place. The ground that was holy once before, this ground where God spoke to Abraham, this unworthy Samaritan ground, is holy ground once again. Only the local people don't understand that yet.

Making a long story short, the Samaritans were the spiritual descendants of the northern Kingdom, Israel. Their ancestors had been settled around the old Israelite capital city Samaria after the Assyrians put an end to Israel. Then Jewish missionaries arrived and converted them to Judaism. Taking Judaism seriously, they built their own temple. They obeyed the laws of the Torah. They accepted the books of Moses. They lived like Jews. They worshipped like Jews. They believed like Jews. They considered themselves Jews. But there had been bad blood between ethnic Samaritans and ethnic Judeans ever since the days of Nehemiah, when the Jews who returned from exile in Babylon told their friendly Samaritan neighbors, who were at first happy to see them, to get lost because they were nothing but unworthy half-breeds and fake Jews.

This was a form of elitist racism, by the way: "We don't care if we have the same religion! Your ancestors are not our ancestors! You speak with an accent! Your skin is not quite the same color, your hair, your eyes! You're not from around here! Go away! Don't worship on our mountain! Don't drink out of our well! You must worship in a separate house! You must drink from a separate fountain!"

Hasn't that happened in our own experience as a people? I know it has. I witnessed it happening in South Carolina more than 50 years ago when I asked my parents embarrassing questions about separate water fountains, separate restrooms, and why some people had to sit in the back of the bus. And in some ways, sometimes very subtle ways, and sometimes not so subtle, it still happens today.

But what irony! When the Judeans told the Samaritans that they were going to be separate and not equal, *they* got the best drinking fountain in the Holy Land. They got Jacob's well.

Most Jews would not stopover in a Samaritan town even for a single night, never mind Jacob's well, thank you very much. "We won't drink from their fountain! It's not clean! We have our own good water!" They would rough it in the countryside if they had to do that for the sake of their religious purity.

But the one who levels the playing field before God considers Samaria to be just as good as Galilee and Judea. Sychar is just as good a place to spend the night as Capernaum and Jerusalem. Samaritans are just as good as Judeans and Galileans. And there is that one special consideration here. The well, the fountain, that place that was meant for all people to come and drink. That well is holy ground. It was before, and it will be again.

One Samaritan woman set foot on that holy ground when the time was right. Without warning, Jesus asked her for a drink from the well. He asked out of respect, as a guest, a visitor who did not want to violate boundaries. He knew they would see him as a Galilean Jew. In their eyes, he was the foreigner. But he knew how other Jews treated Samaritans with contempt. In his act of asking the woman for water from the local well he was building a surprising and unexpected bridge, both with her and with her community.

The woman wanted to know why it was that a *Jew* was asking for a drink from a *Samaritan woman*. There was no protocol for this, no precedent, no guidelines. All Samaritans understood that this was *never* supposed to happen to begin with. The fact that it does happen is nothing less than a minor miracle.

The answer Jesus has is that: "If you knew the gift of God and if you knew who you're talking to, *then* you would ask for *living water*." (John 4:10, my paraphrase.)

The woman is practical, pragmatic, and respectful: "Sir, you don't have a bucket. The well is deep. Where do you get your living water? Are *you* greater than *our* ancestor Jacob?" (John 4:11-12, my paraphrase.) One can hear her defiant Samaritan pride rising up in the face of expected Jewish elitism.

Jesus doesn't play the old elitist game. Instead he tells her that everyone who drinks from the well will be thirsty again, but that he will give people water rising from a spring of eternal life. The woman wants this new water. She's doesn't want to keep coming back to the well. It's hard work hauling a heavy jar of water every time you need it, and you need it all the time, all day, every day. It is the stuff of daily of life.

Now, if you're a smart observer, then you'll see that this whole business about good, clean, drinking water from the well has become a lesson about salvation, justification, and free grace. We try to carry our own water in so many different ways to give us life in so many different ways every day. We work so hard to justify ourselves and it never ends. Trying to carry our own eternal salvation around with us everyday becomes hard and tiring work. We are *not* God. We are nothing but frail and weak mortals. This work of justifying ourselves and building our stairways to heaven, this rat race that the American Religious Industrial Establishment forces us into wears us down, beats us down without mercy, dehumanizes us with draconian expectations, and degrades us with demanding religious laws that we can never succeed at obeying, not to mention that it's pointless in the end, because we always get thirsty again and always have to go back for more. (*Which keeps the American Religious Industrial Establishment in business, by the way.*) The water of our self-salvation runs out too soon. It too easily slips between our fingers. It quickly evaporates when life gets tough. Jesus offers God's alternative: living water, free for the asking, no strings attached, no gimmicks, no hoops to jump through, straight from Jesus' own hands. Drink from this water *only once* and you will never be thirsty again.

But the woman at the well doesn't get it yet.

Jesus told her to go and call her husband. She said she has no husband.

"Right you are!" Jesus said. He then gave her a summary of her life. Five husbands have come and gone. Maybe they died, who knows. The guy she's with now is not her husband.

The woman finds this amazing. How does he know? How he knows is not explained to her or to us. She quickly declares him to be a prophet! *And then she picks an argument with him!* It's because he is a Jew, and the argument is about where God is to be worshipped. Is God to be worshipped on the Samaritans' own good holy mountain, or on *that mountain* in Judea where the Temple sits?

Neither! Jesus says. The time is almost here when we'll see true worship of the Father in spirit and truth, *not* on a mountain!

The woman's not sure what to say. This may have been a little over her head, because she says something that is as generic as it is safe. "Well, I know Messiah is coming. He'll explain everything to us." (John 4:25, my paraphrase.)

And then Jesus point blank says, "I am he, the one speaking to you." (John 4:26.)

The woman runs into the town and tells everyone about this, and many believed Jesus was the Messiah because of what she said. In the end we have an image of the whole town telling the woman that they now know that Jesus is in fact the Savior of the world.

Notice how the story doesn't resolve the whole issue of the woman's living arrangement with the man who is not her husband. The story doesn't say she repented, or that her life with the man not her husband was set to rights as Jews then would understand it. The story doesn't even judge her. Quite the opposite! Having stood on holy ground with Jesus, she found she was validated and perhaps in some way vindicated when the people of the town told her that they believed as she did, that Jesus is the Savior of the world.

In the Eastern Orthodox Church they call her St. Photini, the Woman of Light, and they say she was "equal to the Apostles," because she made the light of Christ known to so many people, starting with the people of Sychar, and finally ending her own Lenten journey in Rome as a Christian martyr. Who knows how accurate the tradition really is. But isn't it just like God to take someone we'd least expect and turn that person into a bearer of the light of Christ? Wouldn't it be exactly like God to take someone who was not allowed to drink from the same fountain as the sacred crowd and turn that person into an apostle who carries the light of Christ back to the sacred crowd as well as to all those who, like her, have been shut out of the sacred crowd?

God is the one who delights in taking the person who is separate and not equal and saying, "The separate well that you drink from is holy ground. Receive the living water of life as a gift, and live as a newly recreated person, someone who may see the Kingdom."

In our Lenten walk with Jesus, as we head toward the cross of Good Friday, we pass by Jacob's well, that holy ground where God takes the nameless and unworthy and turns them into bearers of light for the sake of world. Only the God who loves the world so much that he gave his only Son to the world as a living sacrifice would do this.

Only the God who is the embodiment of love would do this for our sake.

Only the Son, who embodies the God of love would follow this Lenten journey all the way, from Jacob's well to the cross, there to die for our sakes. And so the first call we hear on our Lenten journey today is the call to receive the living water of Christ which is freely given with his own hands to us as a gift of life for our sake.

The second call we hear on our journey today is a call to us as a faith community to rise up and *be* the people who bear the light of this Christ who dies for the world. Take this light to all the world! That is a mission to intentionally seek out the unworthy, the people who must drink from a different well, the people who are separate and unequal, the people who stand on unworthy ground that is truly holy ground, and offer them the living water of Christ with our own hands.

Peace be with you!

THIRD MIDWEEK IN LENT

God Is Like A Precocious Preschooler

Romans 5:1-11

The Apostle Paul had the unique, or, if you prefer, the annoying habit of being able to pack a ton of stuff into just a few statements. The two paragraphs of the reading present a wicked loaded package for us, including:

> Justification.
>
> Grace.
>
> Character.
>
> Love.
>
> Sinners.
>
> Wrath.
>
> Reconciliation.

Those are just a few of the loaded words that Paul throws at us tonight. They make fodder for multiple homilies. What are we to make of this? To steal a phrase Paul uses, "What then are we to say about these things?" (Romans 8:31.) With all the stuff Paul throws at us, we're not even sure where to begin. Not to mention that tonight our visit to the Romans is just another brief stop over on our Lenten journey. Do we even have time for Paul and his heavy, ponderous, loaded thoughts?

Well, maybe not all of them, but if we take only one or two, then we might have a little time for Paul tonight.

The opening words of the reading provide a clue for our focus tonight. "Therefore, since we are justified by faith, we have peace with God through our Lord Jesus Christ,..." (Romans 5:1a.)

This is Paul's central thought, his main point tonight, and his main theme throughout the letter to the Romans. This sounds good to us. We are set to rights with God by faith. We have peace with God through Jesus Christ. All good things. And Paul develops that thought in the reading we had two weeks ago; and don't ask why the lectionary reversed the order of the readings. Sometimes the group mind of the Consultation on Common Texts is beyond human understanding.

What verse one is all about is that we are made right with God without all the stuff that the great Religious Industrial Establishment would want to burden us with. Remember the homily from two weeks back: Paul tells us to toss all that stuff out the window and just trust God.

OK. This is good. Trust God, and we are justified by faith, like Abraham, and this is a gift, grace, that we have through Christ. And if you are a smart reader, and you remember to use your handy dandy Greek reading glasses, you'll see that there is no "obtaining access to" this grace, contrary to the use of that word "obtain" in the lectionary reading. Paul does not use the word "obtain" in the actual Romans text. In Paul's mind, we "obtain" nothing, because that would amount to active self-salvation on our part. What Paul actually says, his own words in the Greek text here, is that through Christ, "we also have, by faith, the condition-of-being-brought-together into this grace in which we stand." (Romans 5:2, my translation.)

Paul credits Christ with much, and he credits passive trust with much as well. Trusting in Christ, we are brought by him ("through him") into the grace of God in which we stand.

What the Dickens is that? Who can give us a really good, understandable, working definition of grace? Modern Christians have trouble with that when they are pressed about it. Even us Lutherans, who teach justification by grace through faith apart from the works of the law.

In the popular use of the word today, "grace" seems to be understood as living in a sort of state of mindless bliss. It seems to be taken as a condition in which we sort of float through life without setting foot on solid ground, a condition in which one is "blessed" because nothing is wrong and all is always right with the world. And in this imagined state of "blessedness" and "grace" we shall be ever blind to the problems that abound in real life. But that strikes me as being just plain *weird*, out of touch with reality, and delusional in the true sense of the word. That's *not* the grace that Paul knew and wanted to tell us about.

Grace, as Paul knew it, was the quality of a gracious God, a God who dwelt in "graciousness." But what was that about? Grace, as the word was used in Paul's society and as Paul would have known it, had to do with the *joy and delight experienced in a great festival* that was held for a specific reason.

For Paul, the grace of God was all about the joy and delight of God. It was something that had a cause and it had to be shared and expressed by God as a great celebration of immense joy. (*Let's recall the great Messianic feast of Isaiah on the mountain of God!*) And the cause of this immense joy was not something that we fragile weak mortals have done or ever could do. It was something that only God could do and has done.

Think of the precocious preschooler who sneaks cookies out of the kitchen and then experiences immense joy and delight because he or she has done this, has to celebrate, and brags to little brother or sister or friends about the great epic and unforgettable deed. (I think we could name a few of those precocious preschoolers. You see, we have living sermon illustrations about the character of God in our midst! Who would have thought it?)

God is like that precocious preschooler. God has done something, and God is incredibly delighted in having done it, and news of it has to be shared! It has to be expressed! It compels us to celebrate! And *what* has God done that provokes this incredible unrestrained delight that has to be shared?

What God has done is to perform a whole series of concrete

demonstrations of salvation throughout the whole history of Abraham and his descendants leading up to the crucifixion of God's own Son and God's reclaiming of the entire cosmos through that final act.

And God pulls off this feat despite the odds, despite sin and death, despite that fact that we were still "enemies," as Paul puts it, because, "For if while we were enemies, we were reconciled to God through the death of his Son, much more surely, having been reconciled, will we be saved by his life." (Romans 5:10.)

And this is the grace of God, the immense, boundless, unlike-anything-that-has-ever-been celebration of God's joy that we have been brought to stand in by Christ, the one in whom we have trusted.

It's something that demands a very different kind of Lenten response from us than tradition dictates, because it demands a great celebration. This is not a celebration that is blind to the condition of the world. It is not one in which we walk about in mindless bliss bearing empty smiles on our faces.

No! It is a celebration that goes out into the streets of the community (*think ahead to Pentecost here, guys*). It goes out to the people who still live in darkness and have not heard about the God who delights in their salvation. It is a celebration that is expressed in bringing the Kingdom near to others by extending to them the hand of Christ even while they are still strangers to Christ, indeed, even while they are still enemies of Christ. And we do this for the sake of the world, by Christ's own command, baptizing and teaching all peoples, so that we may all join in with the great celebration of God's immense and unbounded joy brought about by Christ who died for our sakes.

Peace be with you!

FOURTH SUNDAY IN LENT

The Man Who Can See

John 9:1-41

What a far out Gospel reading we have today! My first thought is that the treatment that Dr. Jesus, the Ophthalmologist of Nazareth, gives to the blind man is not the sort to inspire confidence in his ability to heal, and I'm in no hurry to schedule my next eye exam with him. I mean, mud and spit in the eye! Come on! He wouldn't make it out of medical school today!

My second thought about the reading is that this kind of treatment was common back then when dealing with rabbis and Jewish faith healers who worked to heal common people. Mud and spit were par for the course and were to be expected as needed. The common peasants put up with this because they didn't know any better and because they couldn't afford the professional doctors trained in Greek and Roman schools, who weren't much better anyway. The peasants were desperate to be healed of whatever ailment they had, and mud and spit worked just as well as any other medicine. Besides, the mud-and-spit treatment was probably less toxic than many of the medicinal concoctions cooked up by Greek and Roman doctors in any case.

(As an aside, and this nothing to do with the text, did you hear that the Romans came within a hair of inventing gun powder? Do you know how that happened? A Roman doctor was looking for a cure for what might have been the common cold, and he did this by trial and error, using all kinds of different substances in varying quantities and proportions. In one of his experiments he ground together charcoal, sulfur, and saltpeter. Do you know what that is? He didn't. He started to heat the mix over a fire and...BOOM! It killed him. Because he kept records of his work, we know that he had mixed together the ingredients for gunpowder. One of his colleagues attempted to duplicate his work to see where he went wrong, and...BOOM! So, after two Roman doctors bought the farm, no one attempted to work with those ingredients again because they were just too dangerous for use in the field of medicine. Fortunately, the Roman army never noticed that there might be something the doctors had stumbled on that could have military applications, otherwise we might all be speaking Latin today. Meanwhile, the spit-and-mud approach to medicine was the less explosive alternative.)

This leads to other thoughts, such as:

The method of healing that Jesus uses in this story is not really important. There were plenty of people slopping spit and mud onto blind eyes. That didn't make any of them the Messiah. We shouldn't get so caught up in the method of healing. There's more to the Gospel story than that. But we will come back to the image of mud later.

And, another thought - the important thing in the story is that the man was healed. He received his sight. Jesus sent him to the Pool of Siloam outside Jerusalem's walls, the pool whose name in Hebrew means "Release," "Launching Forth," and "Sending." "Sent" was a sort of rough translation that John provided for his Greek readers, but it's close enough. It is, actually, a variation on the Hebrew word for "Apostle." And that's going to prove to be important. Upon washing the mud away at the Pool of Sending, and yes, there's an allusion to baptism here, the Man Blind From Birth found that he was now the Man Who Can See.

And then he found that he could not escape notice. This led to lots of awkward questions, and then allegations, and finally the Religious Industrial Establishment, the Pharisees, got involved. Clearly, something involving God had happened, but it happened outside of the Pharisees' control, and they could not allow that.

That, in turn, led to a weird, lopsided, convoluted debate in which the learned, professionally trained Pharisees tried to debate with an apparently uneducated man. They tried to get him to deny that what had happened to him had really happened, and then, if healing did in fact happen, then the healer must be a sinner, because he healed on the Sabbath, so the healing itself would be invalidated, as if Jesus could or would take it back!

One expects the Man Formerly Known as Blind to be indignant with the Pharisees. "What do you expect of me? Do you *want* me to be blind, so *your law* will remain unscathed?" What do they want the Man Formerly Known as Blind to do? Do they want him to run back to Jesus and say, "Take it back! You made a mistake! It's the wrong day! Check your calendar! Make me blind again and I'll come back on Wednesday so we can do it right!"

But the Man Formerly Known as Blind holds his ground. He is now the Man ho Can See and he will not deny the reality of his healing. This is an act of defiance to the Pharisees' authority, and so they forcibly drive him out of the synagogue.

And then Jesus gets involved in the story again when he finds the Man Who Can See. The story then moves to its conclusion with a collection of key statements which are reminiscent of a catechism. We can paraphrase it this way:

"Do you believe in, do you *trust* the Son of Man?"

"Who is he? Tell me. I'll believe in him. I'll trust him."

"You have seen him, you know." Recall Jesus talking to Nicodemus about those who see the Kingdom. "You have seen him. I'm that guy."

And then the Man Who Can See responded, "Lord, I believe." Think ahead now to Thomas who sees the risen Lord and his exclamation, "My Lord and my God!" (John 20:28.)

And then, as if to explain what he has done, Jesus says, "I came into this world for judgment so that those who do not see may see, and those who do see may become blind." (John 9:39.) with these words, Jesus indicates that he has come to initiate a complete reordering of this world. His goal is to turn the world upside down. This is the fulfillment of the magnificat, where Mary sings out:

   He has brought down the powerful from their thrones,

> and lifted up the lowly;
> he has filled the hungry with good things,
> > and sent the rich away empty.
> He has helped his servant Israel,
> > in remembrance of his mercy,
> according to the promise made to our ancestors,
> > to Abraham and his descendants forever. (Luke 1:52-55.)

In his healing of the blind man, Jesus has shown that God has returned to fulfill his promise of mercy for the descendants of Abraham. He has shown through a practical act of healing, that God is acting to set this world to rights. Let the world know that God is doing this through Jesus. Let everyone know that God is doing this by setting people to rights, whatever their trouble, and the concrete visible sign of this is the healing of the blind man.

That is a sign that the Pharisees of all times and all places cannot control and cannot explain away. Because they try to do that, and because they are very much aware of what they are doing, Jesus makes reference to their ability to see. Think back to Genesis, when Adam and Eve eat of the Tree of Knowledge of Good and Evil. Having eaten from the tree they are able to see, and so they have lost their innocence. The Pharisees can see what they are doing. They know what they are doing. They are not innocent. Their sin stands firmly in place. By contrast it is the Man Who Can See who is set to rights, made right with God, and justified by Jesus before God.

But there's still more in the reading than that.

The Man Who Can See, the Man Formerly Known as Blind from birth, has more significance for us. The mud Jesus places on his unseeing eyes and the man's blindness both bring to mind the images of Genesis, where God creates humans out of the proverbial mud (the Hebrew of Genesis uses the word *adamah*, dirt, earth, land,...) and, as already mentioned, those people are said to be blind until their eyes are opened by eating from the Tree of Knowledge of Good and Evil.

When the man washes the mud away at Siloam, he does so in a pool whose name has meanings such as "Release," "Launching

Forth," and "Sending." There at the Pool of Release, he finds that he has been released from his blindness. He has been released from his old life spent in darkness and his separation from both God and from those who were nearest to him.

But it gets deeper than that. With the mud Jesus used for healing, he has done nothing less than recreate this man and give him new life, just as God first created humans from the proverbial mud and gave them life in the beginning.

At the pool, by the command of Jesus, the man washes away that mud, that unwanted exterior covering. It is like a baptism with its image of water as the washing away of the sin and corruption that covers us and separates us from God and one another. Then the Man Formerly Known as Blind is launched forth into a new life, recreated, not from nothing, but from the previously existing broken life that had been his, an old life that is now transformed into a new life of light and compassion.

That new life includes new vision because his eyes have been opened. Again, the image of Genesis is recalled here, but it is now different. Where in Genesis people's eyes are opened because of disobedience to the command of God, with negative consequences, here the blind man's eyes are opened as he acts in obedience to the command of Jesus. Instead of gaining the knowledge of good and evil, sin, alienation, and death, he gains compassion and grace, healing and life. This story is about a reversal of the Genesis story. This is what Jesus is about, this Living Word who was sent into the world to redeem the world and set creation back to its intended shape in the image of God.

And then, released from his old life, launched forth into a new life in the light of Christ, the Man Formerly Known as Blind finds he is sent out as the Man Who Can See. It is stretching the name of the pool, but not too much, to say that it is the Pool of Apostles, those who are sent forth. The Man Who Can See is now an apostle, not because he wanted to be one, not because he asked, not because he was good enough, but because he was healed, and he cannot escape notice. The world comes to him, and he can only tell the world what happened:

He was healed. He can now see. (Those who are born from above may see the Kingdom!)

He now has vision springing from a mighty act of God in his life.

He now has a life rooted in what Christ has done for him.

And yes, Jesus did it, an act of mercy unbidden, an act of compassion unearned, and an act of salvation unmerited for one who was totally helpless and passive in the face of the blindness that had alienated him from human community and from God.

John tells us this story so that we might believe and trust Jesus. He says so at the end of the Gospel bearing his name. That's why the Gospel of John was written in the first place.

John wants us to hear this particular story so that we may see ourselves in the Man Formerly Known as Blind, now known as the Man Who Can See.

John wants us to see that man's story as our story.

John wants us to see in this story that this is how Jesus relates to us, the people who do not see today.

This is how Jesus comes upon us where ever we are.

This is how Jesus comes to us as we sit helpless and unseeing in our darkness, not knowing him until he acts in our life.

This is how Jesus gives us sight that we may see the Kingdom.

This is how Jesus acts to recreate us.

This is how we are washed at his command, in the healing waters of a holy place on holy ground.

This is how we may find in those healing waters and by the command of Christ a boundless new life of light and sight as our old life is been recreated in his name.

And this is how we may be sent forth, like the Man Who Can See, in Christ's name, as apostles who bear a transforming witness to the world about what Christ does for the sake of the world, so that the rest of the world may also be healed of its blindness, receive its sight, and see the Kingdom.

Peace be with you!

FOURTH MIDWEEK IN LENT

Shadows of Death, Children of Light

Ephesians 5:8-14

As Paul's letters go, Ephesians is aggravating for many Bible students. I mean, there's no personal names, no specifics about certain problems, that kind of thing. What we do get, however, are remarks like those in tonight's reading, beginning with, "For once you were darkness" (Ephesians 5:8a) and ending with, "Christ will shine on you." (Ephesians 5:14b.)

What are we to do with this reading? ("What then are we to say about these things?" (Romans 8:31.)) We shy away from the long readings because they're overwhelming. But then we come to short readings like this one and we feel that we don't have enough to talk about.

But we do know enough about Ephesians that we have a pretty good idea what it's about. One or two generations after Paul, the church in Ephesus would be known as a church with a mission and a plan, the church of the Elder Apostle John, bearing the light of Christ in the world for the sake of the world. But at the time of Paul, Ephesus was a small faith community that he had scrapped together during the two years he was in the city. It was a small congregation. And it suffered from some of the problems that hold back all small congregations.

We can tell from the way Paul talks to the Ephesians that this was a small church suffering from a sense of powerlessness, helplessness, instability, and a lack of resolve. All of that was caused by an incomplete sense of identity. The Ephesians were wondering who they were as a Christian faith community. Never mind a mission plan. Never mind a five-year plan. Plans are good. We need them if we are to succeed in doing mission. But Paul doesn't give them any plan. They aren't ready for that yet. They still need to have a clear sense of who they are before they can even begin to do mission.

This is exactly the kind of thing we deal with in intentional interim ministry, in which we intentionally work on a congregation's sense of identity. Paul dealt with the Ephesians' sense of congregational identity by starting with the basics and telling the Ephesian Christians who they once were, and who they are now.

One way to translate his opening words in Ephesians 5:8 is like this: "*Once you-guys were shadow people.*" *Shadow people.* Now it starts to get interesting. Let's allow ourselves look at what's in the back of Paul's mind as he speaks to the Ephesians. We can find what he's probably thinking of in Isaiah (9:2), a text Paul would have known well, where it says,

> "The people that walked in darkness have seen a great light. They who sit in the land of the shadow of death, light has shined on them." (My paraphrase.)

The image of sitting in the land of the shadow of death comes from Jewish tradition concerning death and mourning. Isaiah even uses a word that is found in the tradition of "sitting *shiva.*" If you don't know what that is, it's easy to get. If you are Jewish, when someone in your immediate family dies, then the tradition was (and still is for some Jews) that you "sit *shiva*" in your home immediately after the funeral for seven days. The tradition had you sit as close to the floor, or the ground as you could, as close as possible. The point is to be as low as possible, as low as death itself. And then basically you don't do anything for seven days. This is a form of mourning, and during that time your life is reduced to a minimal sort of existence. This was especially true at the time of Paul. You weren't allowed to cook for yourself; friends and neighbors brought you food. You were not allowed to work or conduct business except in specially prescribed situations. You did not go out of the house. You didn't call upon your neighbors for help. You didn't do *anything.* That's not living is it? And that's the whole point. You were dwelling in the land of the shadows of death for seven days. You were one of the shadow people, one step away from being the kind of people Jews believed dwelt in Sheol, all the deceased people of the world who dwelt in the land of death.

The whole thing is depressing, isn't it? But there were a couple of bright spots in this gloomy (and powerful) tradition. It was, and still is, considered an act of compassion to visit a home where the family is sitting *shiva*, and to provide food and company for the mourners. And in visiting that home, it's considered an act of compassion to deliver a blessing:

"May God comfort you,...and may you have no more sorrow."

For some people today that blessing might not mean much; it's just nice words. But for others, those words are powerful and they mean the world. And better than that, your seven days of sitting in darkness could end immediately if a holy day occurred during that time. A "holy day" in Hebrew is literally a "good day" (*yom tov*), and a good day brings with it good news.

Paul writes to the Ephesians as if they have been, and maybe still are, sitting *shiva*, sitting in darkness, living a minimal life. They were the shadow people. They may as well be dead. But there is still good news for them!

Returning to Isaiah, we see that the prophet said the people sitting in darkness have seen a great light, and so Paul delivers a *shiva* blessing to the people who were sitting in darkness, and who need to hear that their dark time is over. He emphatically tells the Ephesians,

<u>Now</u> *you-guys are in the light of the Lord;...*

This is who you are! You no longer sit in gloom!

You no longer live like you used to live!

You no longer live a minimal existence!

You no longer are powerless!

Your faith community no longer needs to sit in one place,

motionless, as low as death itself, stagnating, and dying!

You no longer walk in darkness!

Paul plays off of Isaiah 9:2 here ("The people who walked in darkness have seen a great light.") when he says,

> "*You-guys are now in the light of the Lord;...so you-guys walk as children of the light!*" (Ephesians 5:8b, my paraphrase.)

It's easy for a lot of preaching to go off into the realm of moralizing here. And Paul does caution the Ephesians about what he calls the "unfruitful works of darkness," that problematic, unhelpful *stuff* we get into when we give in to despair in the darkness. There is an appropriate time and place for that kind of instruction. Tonight, however, we are about proclaiming the Good News in the middle of Lent, a time when we Lutherans traditionally sit our own version of *shiva*, sitting in our own darkness, contemplating our own sin, our own failures, our own unworthiness, and truly needing to hear the Good News. In verse 8 Paul has proclaimed the Good News to the Ephesians:

> "*You-guys are now in the light of the Lord;...so you-guys walk as children of the light!*" (Ephesians 5:8b, my paraphrase.)

We are not so different from the Ephesian church. We are small. We have our struggles. We have a temptation to stay sitting in our house, as if we sit *shiva*, forsaking contact with our neighbors. But this is not what Christ wants of us. This is not why Christ died on his cross for us. This is not why his tomb was left empty for us. Paul himself would tell us:

> "*You-guys are now in the light of the Lord;...so you-guys walk as children of the light!*" (Ephesians 5:8b, my paraphrase.)

Great change comes with the light, and now that the light has come, we will never be the same again. We have a future, a vast future in some regards, because we are the people of light right now, today. Our sins, whatever they are, are forgiven in Christ. Our past is dead and buried. Now we are alive in Christ, so, you-guys walk as children of the light. Now, Ephesus, now, Gloria Dei, now, today, this moment, live as the faith community that Christ has called us to be.

"Awake, sleeper, and rise up from the dead, and Christ will shine upon you!" (Ephesians 5:14b, my paraphrase.)

Peace be with you!

FIFTH SUNDAY IN LENT

Lazarus

John 11:1-45

Today we find Jesus on the east bank of the Jordan River. Back in John chapter 10 we are told that he left Jerusalem and was staying at the place where John the Baptist had baptized people "in the early days," as the text says. Although many people came to see Jesus there, as they appear to do everywhere, he's not on a planned, intentional mission journey across the Jordan. This is Jesus in exile.

Jesus has fled from Jerusalem and Judea because of his arguments with the priests at the Temple during Hanukah, the Feast of Dedication. Priests were accusing him of blasphemy and Caiaphas led a faction that wanted to kill him. So, even though it was winter, off he went with his disciples. The ever-present anonymous crowd of followers would be trailing behind him as he set out across the Jordan River, out of reach of those who wanted to harm him. Out of sight and out of mind…for a while.

But Mary and Martha, the sisters of Lazarus, knew where to find him. They sent a messenger to him. The words of the messenger seem calm, "Lord, behold, he whom you love-as-family is sick." (John 11:3, my translation. The word used for love in the text is the word for familial love.) But the underlying feeling of the message is urgent: "You must return! Now! You must come back to Bethany at once!"

You know, back then Hebrew names had meaning. People's names, Mary and Martha, Lazarus, even Jesus, all these names had meaning. Even the names of towns, like Jerusalem, Bethany, all these places had meanings that came to mind when people spoke those names. Sometimes the meanings come into play in the background of the gospel stories.

Bethany meant House of Affliction. Kind of depressing, isn't it? Really makes you want to live there - *not*! If that were the name of south Knoxville, then people would be moving away in droves, and woe to those who stayed!

That Hebrew word for affliction had the double meaning of poverty and illness. Today New Testament experts have reason to think there was an alms house there and a sort of hospital (the two of them may have been one and the same establishment), and between them that's how the town got its name. Anyway, that name, House of Affliction, makes it a convenient and appropriate setting for what happens in the gospel reading today. You see, the home town of Lazarus, the House of Affliction, is where we find Lazarus afflicted with illness and then death. It is where we find his family afflicted with immense grief and deep sorrow.

Ironically, Bethany was also a town within sight of large groves of trees, fig and olive trees, almond and carob trees. The House of Affliction, of poverty and illness, and in the case of Lazarus, the place of death, was surrounded by signs of life and abundance. The first generation or two of Christians who heard this story would have known this, especially if they lived in Jerusalem and the nearby area. They would have seen a powerful image in the story, a deeply compelling image of pain, illness, and death surrounded by thriving abundant life, which is the sign of God's good creation.

That sign is a sign that something in this world has got to change. That sign is one that tells the world that the powers of death and destruction cannot and should not be allowed to continue as they are, that God's will, which is being enacted on this earth by Jesus, the living Word of creation, will not allow death and destruction to continue. What do you guys think? (Deep stuff, isn't it? But really *good* stuff!)

It takes a little persuading, but Jesus decides to return to Bethany. The situation does not look good. Thomas is not optimistic, and expects to die along with Jesus when they return to Judea. There are, after all people in high places in Judea who want to kill Jesus.

His mood only enhances the dark atmosphere of death that Jesus is walking into, the atmosphere of doom which surrounds Lazarus as he lies in the tomb.

Upon arriving at Bethany the situation appears even worse. Lazarus is dead. He has been in his tomb for four days. The sisters Mary and Martha are "sitting shiva" in their home, the Jewish tradition of mourning immediately after the burial of someone in the immediate family. They're been doing that for four days; they have three more days to go. Many people have come to see them, in keeping with the tradition. As an act of compassion for the family we would expect people to bring them food. They would be keeping Mary and Martha company, and bearing words of blessing. When you are practicing this tradition, you're not supposed to leave your house, except for the most important reasons. Remember, I talked about this on Wednesday night in connection with last Sunday's Ephesians reading - where you least expected it to come up!

Martha is told that Jesus and his followers are coming. She breaks tradition and runs out of the house to meet him. (Mary, of course, the one with the reputation for sticking to the rules and playing out by the book her traditional role as a woman of the household and member of the family, stays in the home.)

And Martha is resigned when she meets Jesus. The sense of what she says to Jesus is: "OK, you're here now, but you're too late. It's all over and done with. If you had been here, my brother would still be alive. But I know that God will still give to you whatever you ask." That last remark was an expression of some small sign of hopefulness, but... Was she trying to convince herself? Maybe she doesn't know what to expect now. We would expect her to be in shock at her brother's sudden death. And what does she know of Jesus? Jesus has healed people. He has fed people. He has said some bold things. He has done some bold things. He has made some incredible signs pointing to the Kingdom of God. But he has never confronted death head on. Martha could not expect that he would be able to tackle this one.

In response, Jesus promised her that her brother would "rise again."

Martha then responded with the main Jewish teaching at the time. (That's known as Second Temple Eschatology today.) She said, "I know he will rise again in the resurrection on the last day." (John 11:24.)

Jesus responded to her in a way that appears to contradict the standard Jewish teaching when he said, "I am the resurrection and the life. Those who believe in me, even though they die, will live, and everyone who lives and believes in me will never die. Do you believe this?" (John 11:25-26.)

I don't think Martha expected that response, because the sense of what she says next is kind of like, "Oooooo-kay. Sure. Whatever you say. Yes, Lord. I believe that you are the Messiah, the Son of God, the one coming into the world." It seems like a safe answer under the circumstances, right?

And then the scene repeats itself when Martha gets Mary to break the *shiva* tradition and leave the house and there is a lot of weeping at the feet of Jesus. Everybody's weeping. Our text says that Jesus was "greatly disturbed in spirit and deeply moved" by all this weeping (John 11:33). The New International Version says Jesus was "deeply moved in spirit," and other versions of the Bible say similar things. And you know what? None of them give us the straight translation because they're all trying to sound holy and portray Jesus in some sort of stereotypical, religiously tame and acceptable "Godly" manner.

What text of John really says (in New Testament Greek) is that Jesus "was incomprehensible" and "was struck" by what he was confronted with. In other words, he was *absolutely enraged*! I mean, if this was one of the Marvel superhero movies, this would be the scene where the mild mannered, meek scientist turns into the big green guy and starts smashing things.

Maybe it was all the weeping that finally did it, that intense display of utter human despair and total hopelessness, but Jesus has absolutely had it. These are the people that Jesus has had compassion for, that he has loved as family, and they are being destroyed by death right in front of him. Hunger, poverty, illness, blindness, disability, petty human judgment, sin, ignorance, injustice, rejection, Jesus has confronted all of these things up till now and he has won. But this is the last straw! This is the final line in the sand and the true enemy has had the arrogance to cross it.

Jesus is absolutely enraged, more so than when he threw the money changers out of the temple. He is so enraged he can't contain it. He is enraged to the point of tears, to the point where he can't think straight, where he can't speak clearly ("incomprehensible"), where he absolutely has to *do something*. I mean, this is truly murderous rage. We are not used to thinking of Jesus that way, and that's probably why timid Bible translators water down the text here.

And Jesus is not enraged at the people. They are not his enemy. The enemy is death itself, and it is celebrating now in the tears of the people and it is laughing at him now. It is flaunting itself in front of Jesus and everybody as if it were a petty tin-plated god, and it is mocking Jesus in the words of those who are lost in despair: "Could not he who opened the eyes of the blind man have kept this man from dying?" And he has absolutely had it.

It's in this intense emotional state that Jesus goes to the tomb and takes charge in what is probably one of the most powerful scenes in all four gospels. He commands the stone to be removed: *Get it out of my way!* Who is going to defy him when one can hear the absolute rage in his voice, the total wrath of God that says there is going to be a furious reordering of things here.

His remark, "Did I not tell you that if you believed, you would see the glory of God?" (John 11:40.) is made in that intense emotional setting, and may best be understood as something like, *"You want to see the glory of God? I'll show you the glory of God!"* Then the Gospel of John inserts a nice, calm prayer into the text that doesn't seem to fit into the emotional context of the scene, after which Jesus shouts out, and commands Lazarus with a voice loud enough to wake the dead:

"Hey Lazarus, come out here!" (John 11:43, my translation.)

And against the odds, against all probability, the enemy showed his weakness and retreated when the Living Word of God spoke, and so Lazarus came out of the tomb. Then Jesus commanded the people, and in doing so he indirectly commanded death itself, to unbind Lazarus, and let him go. There at the House of Affliction, at the place of illness and death, death was defeated. Life reigned. And it is implied that in this act the glory of God was seen by a humanity that was previously in despair because it was under immediate threat by death's destruction.

And then, after that,...wow. What are we to say?

The Gospel of John was written so that we may believe. OK. In that case what are we to believe after reading this story? What do you think as we come near the end of our Lenten journey?

I'll tell you what I think, and you can disagree, I don't care. I think we've already touched on it earlier in the homily. Something in this world has got to change. God created the cosmos as something good and abounding in life. That good creation is threatened in a way that the Bible connects to human rebellion against God. But the will of God is that the powers of death and destruction cannot and will not be allowed to continue as they are.

That is why Jesus comes as "the Son of God, the one coming into the world." That is why Jesus is the Living Word that God sent into the world. The Living Word that was present at creation has entered deeply into creation because God so loved the world that God had created, and desired not to condemn the world, but to save the world from death and destruction.

And so Jesus comes into the midst of our lives and enters into our Place of Affliction. He steps into the midst of all our pain, our illness, and our death. He comes to stand amid all the things that threaten to destroy us, and there he speaks as the Living Word of God bringing about new creation. He begins his new creation with us and our present lives, making us live again as newly created humans. He recreates us not out of nothing, but out of our old lives and our old selves, in whatever condition we are currently in, unbinding us from our present and setting us free from our past to live for the future in the glory and the compassion of God.

Well, that's just a few of my thoughts about the reading. What do you guys think? I know you have a few thoughts of your own. It's all deep stuff, isn't it, the Gospel of John, and this story of victory over death. But it's really *good* stuff, the stuff of Good News! The stuff that compels us to share it with others.

Peace be with you!

FIFTH MIDWEEK IN LENT

Flesh and Spirit and...

Romans 8:6-11

Once, years ago, when I was president of an interfaith council in the Great White North, I ran into a young guy from an independent church. Actually, I found him standing in the basement of my church before the confirmation class I was due to teach. We were renting out the basement space to a small new church, and this guy had showed up for their Sunday afternoon service. They were running over time, which most Sundays would not have been a problem, but that day they needed to get out because it was almost time for me to teach my confirmation class and they were in my space. Anyway, I was talking with this person, and I happened to mention the Interfaith Council. I said I thought it would be a good idea for the member faith communities of the Interfaith Council to work together on outreach for the good of all of us. We could pool our resources, help one another do outreach, and everybody would benefit from it. And that triggered quite the response!

This young man started to tell me with great conviction how horrible the Interfaith Council was in the sight of God because the Interfaith Council "accepted gays, Jews, and Muslims." I honestly had no idea what he meant by that remark. It didn't make any sense to me. We had eighteen very different faith communities on the Interfaith Council, mostly Christian, with eighteen different polities, eighteen different theologies, and eighteen different ways of thinking about "gays, Jews, and Muslims." People with a same-gender orientation didn't get any special attention by the council, either good or bad. At that time we simply left the whole LGBT issue alone as a council and let the individual faith communities deal with it in their own ways. We had only one rabbi on the council - he had been around for decades and was one of the founders of the council, and there were no Muslims at all on the council.

When the young man finally ran out of steam I told him that I actually did know something about the Interfaith Council because I was the president of the Interfaith Council. I said, "We do have a rabbi on the Interfaith Council. But we don't have any Muslims. We tried to get the Muslims to come to the table, but so far they're not responsive." (I understand that more recently there is, in fact, a Muslim presence on the council.)

You should have seen the look on his face. It was one of those priceless moments. He had stuck his foot in his mouth big time, and he knew it. Suddenly he whipped out a little tract from his shirt pocket and began proof-texting Romans to me! He wanted to "bring me to Christ" by way of the "Romans road to salvation" because, obviously, as a Lutheran pastor and as president of the Interfaith Council, I must be happily on the road to hell. When I could finally get a word in edgewise, I told him that I already knew about Romans. After all, we Lutherans kind of wrote the book about Romans, after the Apostle Paul. And I have a confirmation class to teach, and your church is leaving now. The pastor of the church renting from us was embarrassed by his behavior and sort of ushered him out then, and life got back to normal at the old Lutheran church at 6th and Columbia Streets.

I think the guy missed the whole point of Paul's letter to the Romans. Many people do. You know they do when they try to turn Romans into book that has the dismantled components of some ultimate legalistic formula for salvation carelessly scattered about and buried within the text, just waiting for the right person to come along and put all the pieces together into a bludgeon to use in battering unsuspecting innocents. But Paul didn't write Romans for people to use it that way. I think he would be horrified to learn that his letter is being picked apart and selectively used in that manner, and I can imagine what he'd say about that. Can you imagine Paul's Letter to the Americans? It would be a real howler.

In tonight's reading, Paul does talk about some things that some people love to use as proof texts. He talks about flesh and Spirit. He talks about life and death, law and righteousness. What's going on? What is Paul presenting to us? Not stepping stones into the Kingdom, that's for sure, but something else.

Paul has set forth things in terms of "flesh" and "Spirit." That was a very Jewish way of talking at the time of the Apostle Paul, and it's a kind of shorthand for saying that one way of living, the way of the "flesh," is concerned with a very selfish, self-centered, narcissistic, toxic way of living and believing. Meanwhile, the way of the "Spirit" was a healthy God-centered way of living and believing in accordance with and at peace with the will of God. That's over-simplifying things, I know, but we do not have much time tonight, so it will have to do.

Part of what Paul is doing here is calling on his own Jewish roots. What he has in mind is Deuteronomy chapter 30, where the text says, "I have set before you today life and death," (v. 15, my paraphrase), and then calls on Israel to obey the commandments of the Lord your God and live, but turn away, and die. (vs. 16-18.)

Paul has equated the "flesh" with death, and the "Spirit" with life. Even more than that, in Paul's mind, the way of "flesh" is the way of sin, the way of narcissistic, destructive rebellion against God and, keeping the lessons of Genesis in mind, not to mention the lessons of Deuteronomy, Paul believes that rebellion against God can only end one way, and that is in the darkness of death.

Has Paul become legalistic on us? There are those who treat Romans as, and use it as, a legalistic book, but I don't think it is. Paul really believes that anything and anyone who is "in the flesh" is doomed to die because of their rebellion against God and the ultimate failure of "the flesh" to keep God's commandments because of sin. But that means the death of everyone! Is Paul going off the deep end? Has he lost it? Is he so pessimistic about humanity that he believes we are all doomed?

Actually, no. Paul balances everything he says about death with talk about the Spirit and life. After painting a dismal picture about life "in the flesh," Paul then proclaims to the Roman Christians that, "you are not in the flesh! You are in the Spirit, because the Spirit of God lives in you!" (Romans 8:9.)

This is the Spirit that Jesus spoke of when he talked with Nicodemus.

This is the Spirit that goes where it will, when it will, and it will dwell within whomever it will.

And it is this Spirit that, for Paul, brings life, not our total obedience to Torah and Law.

That is, I think, where Paul breaks from his Jewish upbringing which taught that the Torah, containing God's commandments, is life. But Paul says the Spirit is life! Where Jews had taught that the Torah and Law must dwell in the believer, Paul says it is Christ and the Spirit that dwells in the believer.

> But if Christ is in you, though the body is dead because of sin, the Spirit is life because of righteousness. If the Spirit of him who raised Jesus from the dead dwells in you, he who raised Christ from the dead will give life to your mortal bodies also through his Spirit that dwells in you. (Romans 8:10-11)

We frail mortals of flesh have no righteousness. Our sin makes that impossible. When it comes to righteousness we are bankrupt, and if we claim otherwise we deceive ourselves and the truth is not in us. But Christ does have righteousness of his own. This is how Paul makes sense out of the problem that he has raised in the reading, and the problem is this:

If we frail mortals of flesh are doomed to die because of our disobedience, then *how* do we live? How do we "see the Kingdom?" How are we put right with God?

Well, by righteousness, of course, Paul would say, in keeping with his Old Testament upbringing.

But what righteousness is this? We have none! We are the flesh he speaks about. All humanity that has ever lived and ever will live are "the flesh" that is doomed to die! And the "flesh that dies" fails at obedience to God. Where does this righteousness come from then? Whose righteousness is it?

God's righteousness is seen in God's faithfulness to God's covenant. Salvation is the ultimate consequence of the unfolding of God's covenant. God's covenant unfolds in the faithfulness of Jesus which leads to an open tomb.

We are put right with, and by, and in, and through Christ, who is the *only one* who ever was and ever will be obedient to God, even obedient to the point of death on the cross as Paul will tell us in Philippians (2:8). His alone is the righteousness that redeems, cleans, heals, restores, forgives, and raises his people from death into new life. His alone was the choice, the decision, and the sacrifice to fulfill God's will on earth as in heaven and bring all the fallen flesh of humanity into God's family.

And this is the Good News from Paul for the Romans, for us, and for the world as we near the end of our Lenten journey this year:

We do not walk the path of our own salvation. We do not carry that burden ourselves. We can't. We are too weak. Too frail. Too mortal. But the One Who Is Obedient has done this! Christ, the Living Word, the embodiment of God, who is in you! For the sake of Christ, the Spirit of God who raised Jesus now dwells in you! And he who raised Christ from the dead will give us life through the Spirit that dwells in us.

Peace be with you!

SUNDAY OF THE PASSION/PALM SUNDAY

Amid the Hosannas and the Palms

Matthew 21:1-11 (Processional Gospel)

&

Matthew 27:11-54 (Passion Gospel, alternate reading)

First thoughts on today's Processional Gospel:

Yosemite Sam riding a donkey that's much too small for him as he yells, "Yah, mule! Yah, mule! Giddy-up, mule!" Those familiar with Yosemite Sam know that it doesn't matter what he happens to be riding, mule, camel, elephant, or old tin Lizzie; his by-word is always, "Yah mule!" Somehow he reminds us of ourselves, plodding through life on our donkey, not sure of where we are going, but trying very hard nevertheless to get there.

Second thoughts on today's Processional Gospel:

Simple Sunday School images of Jesus riding a donkey into Jerusalem under a bright sky. Happy people cheering him on, singing, waving palm branches and throwing them down in his path. A crowd singing, "Hosanna to the Son of David! Blessed is the one who comes in the name of the Lord!" The air is filled with high spirits, innocence and goodness.

First thoughts on today's Passion Gospel:

It's long, and that's the alternate short version. The full text for today has one hundred twenty-three verses. One begins reading the text and about twenty verses into it starts to wonder where it will end. It's more than one person should have to read at one time. Note for future reference: maybe next year I should have a few helpers. With a few adventurous helpers, we can have a dramatic reading of the text.

Second thoughts on the Passion Gospel:

Thirty pieces of silver. Deceit. Frightened disciples. A wooden cross. More pain and agony than even the words of Matthew can capture for us. A tomb. A closed door. Innocence has died. Goodness is shrouded in darkness. The will of God seems to be in retreat.

A major conclusion that one reaches after making these observations: the sermon better be short.

A much more important conclusion we reach after all the readings is that today we begin the remembrance of the week when Jesus went to Jerusalem for the last time. We remember how Jesus gathered his disciples to celebrate the Passover feast and brought them to the upper room of a house in Jerusalem where he took bread, blessed it and broke it and gave it to his disciples and told them this is his body. We remember how he took the cup of wine and also blessed it and shared it with his disciples and told them this is his blood poured out for the forgiveness of sins.

And we remember that he is the one who went to the cross and died for all humanity, sinners and frail, weak, undeserving mortals though we be.

While we plodded along in our life, not sure of where we were going, the Living Word of God had a destination in mind for us.

While we were trying so hard to get somewhere in our life he was being crucified for us.

In his being crucified he was making true salvation a reality for us. He was justifying us. He was putting us in the right before God, and claiming us as his own, so that we would not have to keep trying to win God's freely-given compassion by our own inadequate failing efforts. He alone, without help from us and without our cooperation, accomplished the deed of salvation so that, indeed, we would not have to win salvation through our own failing efforts at all. Anything less and anything else would make Jesus a sham of a Messiah and a failed savior. But it is not the will of God that Jesus fail. This is what the grace of God is about.

On the cross, as the one who embodies God, Jesus has freely and ultimately assured God's saving grace for everyone. He has done this for that world that God has so loved with complete compassion. So complete is his dying deed that *any action* we could possibly take now by way of cooperating with the work of salvation that he has completed would amount to turning our backs on the crucifixion and rejecting God's forgiving and saving grace so that we might trust in our own grace, if we dared to be so arrogant. That would, when you stop to think about it, be a simple and disingenuous repeat of the same old story that began in Genesis, where the serpent told the humans that, through their own action - eating from the tree of knowledge of good and evil, they could be like God if they wanted. And I think that would be the definition of hell, to intentionally have one's back turned to God, especially if one did that by trying to become like God and tried to claim some share in making one's own salvation happen.

But honestly facing the cross where human failings are brought into focus, and there, at the foot of that cross, facing the outpouring of God's will into this world through Christ, we see that Jesus has already redeemed us all from our own sin and death totally and completely.

We see that by entering into the tomb, Jesus allows us to leave the tomb.

We see that by having a door closed in his life, Jesus opens a door to new life for us.

We see that we cannot do any of this, even in part, for ourselves. No one kicking around on this third rock from the sun can do any of this for us – no one but Jesus, the Living Word of God, the one sent into the world to redeem the cosmos because God so loved the world that it had to be so. He was the only one who was obedient to God, even unto death on a cross. Only he can take the ultimate leap of faith, rising on a cross and plunging into the darkness of the abyss for us. Only he, not any past, present, or future version of Caesar, and not any one of us, is the savior of the world with all of its suffering and dying humanity.

With his cross he brings our failed and dying humanity new life. He gives us life as it was meant to be, life in the image of the God of life. With his death he brings us the opportunity to start over. He gives us the chance to begin again. He holds out to us the opportunity to have a new start. With his rising he gives us a clean break from the past and opens up a new future before us on the landscape of his new creation.

This is Good News for everyone of us, who, like Yosemite Sam on his mule, are just plodding along, taking life one step at a time, one day at a time, hoping to get somewhere on our own efforts, and getting nowhere fast on our own. Our own sin, which, for Yosemite Sam, took the form of a grudge against a certain precocious rabbit, always gets in the way, and we never, ever make the goal.

This is Good News because, despite our failure, despite our inability to save ourselves, indeed, even because of our sin and despite our sin, God has given us a vast future, a destiny, a place to be and to belong and to be accepted, even when it seems that innocence has died and goodness is shrouded in darkness.

The one who emptied himself on the cross has filled all humanity with forgiveness for sin and thrown open the doors of God's Kingdom for us, and we only need to be told that this world and our future has changed because of it.

It is perhaps too much to expect for us to take it all in in just one sitting, one sermon, or one Bible study. There are too many doors opening for us to look through them all in one day. There is too much in God's compassion to take hold of at any one time. There is too much in God's salvation to see every destination ahead of us at once. But that, too, is Good News for us, because it means the compassion of God is overwhelming, sweeping forth from the cross at that one place and one moment to flood over all the world, all people, at all times, and in all places.

Today, amid the hosannas and the palms, with the shadow of the cross looming ever closer, we receive the call to let God's compassion overwhelm us for a time, even if it is just a short time, even if it is only a few minutes, that it might spark a change within us, a transfiguration, a new creation, and a new life. And that change, once having caught hold, may then follow God's will and flare up as new life for us, for our congregation, and for our community.

Peace be with you!

MAUNDY THURSDAY

This Night Is Different

Matthew 26:17-30

How is this night different from all other nights?

It might be that we raised that question last year at Maundy Thursday, and that's OK. You can ask this same question every Maundy Thursday, make it a habitual practice, a tradition, but only as long as you actually deal with the question.

Tonight we remember the night that Jesus sat with his disciples in the upper room to celebrate a meal, the Passover Feast. This is the Feast of Unleavened Bread, the feast that recalls the night God set the Israelites free from their slavery in Egypt and set them forth on a journey to the Promised Land.

Did anyone ask Jesus why that night was different from all other nights? No one can know for sure. But Jews have maintained an ancient tradition of asking that question at the Passover meal. The practice is that the youngest person at the table who is able to recite the question would ask it, and this would happen early in the meal.

But why? Why bother? Why ask the same question every Passover at the table of Unleavened Bread? There is a purpose for this. This is the Jewish way of teaching: question and answer, question and answer, back and forth, back and forth.

This is the teacher and the student.

This is Jesus and Nicodemus. Jesus and the Samaritan woman at the well. Jesus and the Pharisees. Jesus and the priests. It is even Jesus and Pontius Pilate.

This is catechism. This is liturgy. This is the Word of God and the faith community in conversation.

This is God and the prophets, God and Abraham, God and God's creation in relationship.

You can go pretty far with that, you know?

And this is good, because the question leads us far. How *is* this night different from all other nights?

For those disciples who were with Jesus, the night was to take an unexpected turn.

Jesus took the bread, gave a blessing, and broke the bread. Then he gave it to his disciples. This was normal during the Passover meal. Right smack in the middle of the meal, the presider takes the unleavened bread, pronounces the Passover blessing, and then breaks the bread, and everyone at the table eats a piece of it. This is what seems to happen in verse 26 except for one thing:

Jesus tells his disciples that this bread is his body! His "whole, entire body," if we stick strictly to Matthew's own wording in the Greek text of the gospel. That means it is *everything* that Jesus is, his whole being, everything that he is about.

This is different. This is new. This is *unprecedented*. And equally strange, I think, is that if the disciples were in any way surprised by this, Matthew doesn't let us know it. Maybe the inner feelings of the disciples weren't that important for Matthew, I mean, their inner feelings about what Jesus said wouldn't change anything, would they? And yet Matthew went out of his way to relate a disturbing conversation between them about who would betray Jesus. It was turning into a strange night for the disciples, a night that was different from all other nights.

Finally, near the end of the meal of Unleavened Bread, there is the final blessing of the Passover meal over the third cup of wine, a common drinking cup. This seems to be when Jesus took a simple, unremarkable cup, a *poterion* in Matthew's text, gave thanks, and said to his disciples, "Drink from it, all of you!"

This would be verse 27. But once again something unusual happens as Jesus breaks from Passover tradition and tells his disciples that this wine is his blood of the covenant, which is poured out for many for the forgiveness of sins. And more than that, he says that he will never drink of this wine again until he drinks it anew in his Father's Kingdom.

One gets the sense that whatever is going down here, it's all or nothing.

And there is no explanation about any of this from Matthew. He only says that they sang "the hymn," which would be the Passover hymn sung after the Passover meal. That would be the *Hallal*, Psalms 113-118. And then they all went to the Mount of Olives.

Matthew is annoyingly and distressingly vague, and perhaps that is intentional. He is not concerned with giving future generations an accurate and historical account of that night. He only wants to make sure we get the basic points, the important stuff, so that we know why this night is different from all other nights.

What makes this night different is that this is the night the Son of God offers up his body of sacrifice. Don't think just in terms of body and blood, and yeah, I know a lot of pain came out of the arguments of the Reformation about the body and blood of Christ, but it is more than that. This is about the sacrifice of absolutely everything that Jesus is, his life, his being, his spirit, his whole body, everything that he is, everything that he stands for, everything that he has done, going out there to be offered up and poured out for many for the forgiveness of sins. Even more than that! In as far as Jesus embodies God, *this is God* going up to be sacrificed in order to fulfill the old covenant with Abraham once and for all.

And that is why this night is different from all other nights.

This is the night that we remember when God sent Jesus, the Lamb of God, who would mark us with his own blood on a cross so that death may pass us over, and our sins, which are many, may be forgiven and forgotten.

This is the night when we remember that he who is righteous interceded for us, that we may be justified by his righteousness.

This is the night when the one who embodies God would stand before those who would condemn him, with no one to intercede on his behalf.

This is the night when we remember that the Light of the World began his descent into the deepest darkness that one could possibly enter into,

...before rising to the highest heights possible in light before the throne of God,

...so that we who were once at odds with God may be set to rights before God by Christ,

...that we who were once in darkness may be lifted up in the light of new creation by Christ,

...that we who were in bondage to sin and death may be set free from our slavery by Christ,

...and set by the one who justifies us within the open gates of the Kingdom of God.

Peace be with you!

Jack A. Wilder

GOOD FRIDAY

Cross, *Kairos*, and New Creation

John 18:1-19:42

During Holy Week, twenty-seven years ago when I was an intern pastor, I learned that my role in the Good Friday service was to carry a cross up and down the aisle while the choir sang an anthem. The cross I was presented with at rehearsal on Wednesday was a four-foot tall, hollow, plastic cross, light as a feather. I could carry that cross all day if I had to, and carry it high.

At rehearsal, my supervisor kept badgering me as I carried the cross down the aisle: "Slow down! Lift it higher! Slow down! Lift it higher!" He wanted a dignified, stately, reverent procession of the cross for this cathedral-sized Chicago church on Good Friday. No problem. This was going to be easy. That was Wednesday afternoon. Then came Friday.

Friday evening I found that my supervisor had changed his mind. Without warning he decided that the dinky plastic cross they had used in the Good Friday service for years and years was no longer good enough. Instead of the plastic cross, I was directed towards another cross, one leaning against the altar. (Key the dramatic revelation music here...) There it was, the mother of all processional crosses. Six feet tall, solid oak, wicked heavy. My cross to bear. I could barely lift it.

This was a disturbing change of plan. I didn't want to do this. I told my supervisor I didn't think this was going to work. Did he listen to me? Oh, no! Why should he listen to me? Just because I know my own limitations? I was nothing but the intern, what did I know?

When the time came, there was absolutely nothing dignified or stately about it. Time seemed to slow down, which I did not want! It was that *kairos* time, that special, holy, dragged out, agonizing time of God when special things happen. Somehow I got that cross down two sets of steps from the altar to the aisle without tripping. Somehow I got that cross down the aisle without dropping it, but it was touch and go. The cross was swaying from side to side with every step. People at the ends of the pews were reaching out to touch it! And I was thinking: "Don't touch it! Don't touch it! One little nudge and it'll go over! It'll flatten everybody in the pew!" And the choir was no help at all! They seemed to sing slower and slower with each step, and my arms were about to fall off, and that cross was sinking lower and lower with every step, and it was a very long aisle. Somehow, by the grace of God, or perhaps sheer determination to show my supervisor that he was not going to win whatever game he was playing, I got that cross all the way back up to the altar, and when I set it down, it went down with a very loud **THUD!** But I had done it! And it was in some way empowering for me to have done it, which means that, somehow, the grace of God was present in that cross, at that time, and at that place.

The cross that Jesus carried and died upon is wrapped up in the grace of God. It is entwined with the grace of God.

   It is permeated with the grace of God.

   It is saturated with the grace of God.

   It is dripping with the grace of God.

It is a cross of recreating grace that God has staked out at a central key point in space and time: the death of the Messiah, the death of the Living Word of God, the death of the physical embodiment of God. The truly faithful and righteous one who embodies the compassion of God has been nailed onto a bloody instrument of execution atop a dusty hill in a backwater third-rate failed nation.

There was nothing romantic about it. There was nothing dignified, or stately, or reverent about it. The best theological minds of the time would never have expected to find God in that scene, especially if God were nailed on the cross itself.

And yet this place where the cross is planted is holy ground. *This* is where humanity stands at a holy time, that *kairos* time of God when time seems to stand still at the edge of eternity. This is the special, agonizing, holy time of God in which God is working things out according to God's will, not our will. And, as a consequence of God's working in this world, the entire cosmos is changed and turned about, despite itself, in accordance with the implacable will of God.

Within that holy time of God, *kairos*, that single point in time when Jesus dies on the cross is *the point* at which our great Sin, with all of its attendant little sins, our great human rebellion and disobedience to God, is forgiven as the one who intercedes for us accepts our failed lives and the consequences of our failure as his own, hands us his own righteousness, and sets us to rights, so that we are set free from our own sin and death.

And do not misunderstand. God does not intend for Jesus to fail as we have failed. The cross may be the ultimate sign of failure in human experience, but for God it is a sign of success. For this world, a cross is the sign of certain and painful death, condemnation, rejection, and failure. But God has God's own way of doing things.

For the God of Abraham, the cross is the sign of ultimate success, because the cross is about new life. It is about reclaiming the lost and bringing them all into the Kingdom. It is the beginning of the new recreated world that God is busy bringing about. The cross is about God saying, "Look, guys, you messed it all up from the very beginning! You ate from that tree at the center of creation because you wanted to be gods yourselves. Talk about ego!"

But now there's a *new tree* at the center of creation: the cross. And around this new tree creation begins to be remade, recreated in God's image as the humans that are touched by the cross are themselves recreated in God's image to live as God's people in God's new world.

It all begins anew, here, now, in this one timeless moment at the cross, where the old covenant is fulfilled so that the new covenant may begin.

It begins with the price for the old covenant, which was broken by all of the fallible mortal humans who ever lived and ever will live, being delivered in full at God's own expense. This is what the covenant with Abraham was all about and what it was always leading up to. With the old covenant fulfilled at the cross, the new covenant begins at the empty tomb.

This is something that defines our faith community. If we are true to who we are as the people who are touched by the cross, and Lutherans have *always* been people of the cross, and if we are people who are being recreated by God through the cross, then the implications for our own faith community are far-reaching.

What the cross means is that our faith community itself *will* change if it is to experience new life. We will change in some ways as a congregation, in constructive ways yet to be discerned, in ways that are in keeping with our denominational stance on Word and Sacrament, in order to remain true to what the cross is about:

> New creation and new life. All of that is in Christ's name. All of that is in the image of God. All of that involves the Christian faith community participating in and working for the sake of the new creation that God is working in our community, right here in Knoxville.

Perhaps that is disturbing for us, because to be given the grace of God is to be *changed, now,* as well as later. And change, as disturbing or as uncomfortable as it may be for some of us, is itself an experience of the grace of God descending upon this world from the cross. But grace does not mean everything is just great and cozy now so we can just linger as we are.

The grace of God means the transforming of our local church into a place of *holy ground*, bringing us into *holy time*, that *kairos* time of God at the edge of eternity, that special, agonizing, dragged out, holy time of God in which God is working things out. As a consequence of God's working in this congregation as well as in the rest of the world, the entire cosmos is changed and is turned about (and turning about is all about repentance!), despite itself, in accordance with the implacable will of God.

Good Friday calls us to consider our willingness to change, to let go of the status quo, and to embrace new creation as the fulfillment of God's will.

That is a serious conversation for this congregation to have as you are trying to figure out how you want to spend the next few years. And if we are astute observers we will see that this conversation has already begun at a grass-roots level, which calls upon us all to begin to consider what new life and new creation means for this congregation.

This is where the cross is leading us, and when that tomb stands empty and its entrance stands open on Easter Sunday, then we will find God's new creation in our face, demanding our attention and awaiting our response.

But first there comes the cross. There, on the cross, the old covenant is fulfilled, at a great, unthinkable, unbearable cost, and Jesus descends into the tomb, leaving us to wait for the coming Son Rise...

Peace be with you!

Jack A. Wilder

EASTER SUNRISE

Among the Graves

Luke 24:1-12

This morning we stand among the graves.

I once taught a girl in my confirmation class who, at the age of fourteen, was smart as a whip. She was musically talented. She was well-read. She could think rationally and theologically. She made top grades in school. She wanted to be a veterinarian. And...she liked to play among the graves at Cedar Park Cemetery in Hudson, New York.

She thought the cemetery was a cool place to hang out, the coolest place in all of Hudson. The mausoleums and monument tombstones were especially cool, because she and a couple of friends could climb on them and dance on top of the mausoleums. Or so she said, and knowing her, I think I believe her. She didn't think it was strange, though most people would. She didn't think it was disrespectful, though other people would. And she wasn't afraid of being caught by the police, though some people would be afraid of that. Dancing about the graves and on top of mausoleums was a sort of natural celebration of life for her, even if a place of death was a strange place to celebrate life. And no, I could never get her to explain why that was so. Teenagers! They can be so hard to understand.

But look at us. Where are we right now? We are in a cemetery this morning. I haven't caught any of you dancing on top of a mausoleum yet, but here we are, a bunch of grown people, just casually hanging out among the graves as if this is the coolest place to be in south Knoxville. Perhaps the people of south Knoxville think we are a little strange because we are out here. *Why* are we here? Are *we* going to dance about the graves?

Once, a deacon was telling me about the difficulty she ran into when she was planning to preach for Holy Week and Easter. It was the first time she had to preach for Easter and she was deeply worried about trying to explain or define or prove the resurrection of Jesus to her congregation. Some people might assume that this is exactly what she is supposed to do. Another deacon made it clear to me that Easter sermons are ridiculously easy. "They preach themselves," he said. In fact both assumptions are wrong.

The truth is that we who preach and we who proclaim and we who have a life of faith are called upon to prove nothing. And the Easter stories do not preach themselves. If you think it is that easy then just tell that to the women who were at the empty tomb. They who went to the disciples and told them the story of their experience would tell us that it was not easy at all.

But the Easter story *does* require a proclamation that brings Good News to the people sitting in the back pews, the people standing in the food lines at the Vestal food pantry on Wednesday, and the people wandering on the backstreets of the city because they have nowhere else to go. And that is not easy. What does it mean to those of us who were not there and have never seen that tomb? What does it mean to us that on one particular day one particular tomb was empty when by all rights it should have been occupied?

This kind of guidance did not help the deacon who had a hard time preaching for Holy Week and Easter. It only made things harder for her. She had developed her own understanding of the empty tomb, which she should do, and her understanding of that empty tomb was deeply mystical and heavily theological. She was then, and still is, very much like a Medieval mystic, somewhat like Julian of Norwich and Meister Eckhart, people who thought very deep thoughts about God and sought a very deep spiritual relationship with God. Now, that's OK, but she wanted to share with her congregation the depth of her mystic insight and spiritual development that she had grown into over years and years of study and reading and reflection and spiritual direction. She wanted to do all of that in just *one sermon*, on Easter morning.

Well, there was a problem with that. We can't take ten years of learning and spiritual growth and cram that into people's heads in just a few minutes with one sermon. We are called upon to do something else. We are called upon to make a proclamation. We who preach and proclaim, and every last one of us who lives a faith life is called upon to make a proclamation to the many who are not at the tomb's entrance. We are called upon to proclaim that "He is not here, but has risen."

But we are not to stop there, because the Easter proclamation does not preach itself. The proclamation that we make is a prophetic proclamation. This proclamation is prophetic because if it has any real meaning at all then it has a real impact on our world, in the midst of our community, where we live. It means something for the real people living in our community. It impacts upon our everyday lives in a basic, deep, and lasting way, a transforming, recreating way. It gives us hope for tomorrow and new life for today when we have been living in so many ways in the shadow of death day after day.

We carry the prophetic proclamation that begins with the words, "He is not here, but has risen." This is the living proclamation that continues by shouting out that "Christ is risen, and life reigns!" And because life reigns, our community can experience renewed, recreated life in Christ.

This means the alienated can be reconciled.

The hungry can be fed.

The homeless can find shelter.

The abused can find protection.

Those who have suffered loss can be restored.

Those who mourn can be comforted.

Those who suffer sadness can know joy.

Our dying and struggling congregations can have new life.

The Kingdom of God can come near to south Knoxville and all its people because the tomb is empty, Christ is risen, and life reigns.

And here we are. Standing in the cemetery. Among the graves. But as we stand here today, we remember that on one particular day one particular grave was empty when it should have been occupied. And we know, because we have been told by those who came before us, some of whose graves may be in this very cemetery, that sin and death and all that is dark in our world has been defeated.

In the open doorway of the empty tomb the compassion of God has triumphed! The freely-given grace of God has seized all the world and holds it close to God! Love wins! Compassion wins! Grace wins! And God moves out of that divine love, compassion, and grace to begin a new creation, the first born of which is the risen Son himself.

Here, among the graves, in the new light of the Son Rise, we welcome the new creation that God is bringing into the world, and we celebrate! Like the morning stars in the book of Job celebrate at the creation of the world, we celebrate at the new creation that the risen Christ signifies. And then we go out from our celebration, out through the open doorway of the tomb into the world, where we proclaim to all our community that:

"He is not here, but has risen! Let us share with you this new life he brings to us all!"

Peace be with you!

Jack A. Wilder

EASTER SUNDAY

Son Rise

Matthew 28:1-10

Matthew's Easter story throws a quick succession of epic images at us:

> Shadowy figures silently exit the city. They proceed to the tombs in the quiet half-light of the new day.
>
> An earthquake shakes the landscape.
>
> A personal "messenger of the Lord" descends from heaven, somewhat like lightning. He rolls back the stone that seals a tomb's entrance.
>
> Armed guards, the symbol of Caesar's power and authority, agents of the ruler of this world, collapse and are helpless.

It doesn't sound exactly like the other Gospel stories of the empty tomb, does it? But this is Matthew's story. He has his own reasons for the way he portrays the story, and we'll respect that. Today, we are members of *his* congregation, nearly two thousand years ago.

The images Matthew uses are images of immense power and authority, even otherworldly power and divine authority. Incredible awe and even fear, outright irrational terror, would be the natural response of the characters to the events portrayed in the scene. It is understandable then, that the "messenger of the Lord" uses the word for "being terrified" when he tells the women not to be afraid. That reassurance is, in fact, necessary because something totally unexpected and wholly without precedent has happened.

What has happened is that the world has changed. It changed

overnight, in the blink of an eye, somewhat like the strike of a lightning flash. The world is going to be forever different now. The past has been redefined in the light of an open tomb. The present day has been reset and made anew. Even the future has been rewritten.

On Maundy Thursday and Good Friday we did something different. It wasn't exactly planned, but the circumstances seemed to demand that we do something different. Instead of the usual, formal homilies we had conversational, back-and-forth, interactive sermons. It seemed to work well with the small groups we had on those nights.

In those conversational sermons we talked about:

> Jesus drinking from the cup anew with his disciples in his Father's Kingdom, pointing us toward God's new creation.
>
> We talked about the cross, and carrying it; how that cross may not be the one we expected or want to carry, and how that changes people.
>
> We talked about how the grace of God is in the cross, and in the changes that come with the cross.
>
> And we talked about newness, and a little bit about what that means for a small congregation like ours.
>
> One last thing we talked about was the command that comes with the telling of the Good News. This command is, "Do not be afraid." We are given this command because change can be undesirable, disturbing, and frightening, even though it comes with and through the grace of God and is very often needed in our lives.

As of this morning, we have passed through the shadows of Lent and left them behind. We have sat through the Last Supper of Maundy Thursday and carried the cross of Good Friday. We stood in a cemetery at sunrise where, with our Presbyterian brothers and sisters, we walked with Mary Magdalene and her companion among the graves.

Now, after all of that, we stand in a place where a stone has been rolled away from the entrance to a tomb. Before an empty tomb we are presented with signs of power and authority. In this place where death has been overthrown by life we are offered reassurance: "Do not be afraid." Our justification before God is guaranteed. We stand on holy ground, where our hearts beat in holy time, in *kairos*, within the time of God.

In Matthew's story of the resurrection of Jesus, we are at a time and a place where the will of God unfolds into this world. Emerging from the empty tomb, God's will spreads outward across the cosmos and turns the universe about, bringing repentance - that God-willed turning about with its change of heart, change of mind, and change of direction, setting everything to rights through Christ crucified, buried, and raised.

In this place God has planted the cross and the tomb at a central key point in time and space, between the past and future, fulfilling the old covenant of the dead past and beginning the new covenant of the living future, the covenant that brings in the Kingdom of God, so that the will of God may be done on earth as in heaven.

"Look here," the messenger of the Lord said to the women. "Here's a sign that the will of God is being done on earth as in heaven. He is not here! He has been raised! Come, see the place where he lay!"

For Mary Magdalene and her companion, otherwise known as "the other Mary," the absence of Jesus in the tomb was a sign of something God had done. Most people take it for granted that this is a sign that death has been defeated and that all the destructive power of death has been overturned by God. All of that is here, of course, but there is more than that at work.

The empty tomb is first and foremost the sign of God's new creation being enacted, "initiated" or "inaugurated," some will say, in the present world, otherwise all talk of death being defeated makes no sense. Rising upward in the midst of this world's death and decline, the New Creation starts with the Son Rise, as the Risen Jesus himself, the one that the Apostle Paul would call in his letter to the Romans "the first born of all creation" (Romans 8:29), is raised among the tombs.

With the Son Rise of the Risen Jesus, creation starts all over again. It starts again, not from scratch, and not out of nothing, but out of the old, dying world itself. With the living Christ who leaves the tomb empty, God is actively resurrecting the dying world and recreating the old world *now, today,* under our noses, in the image of God that it was meant to bear in the beginning.

I know, it's heavy stuff for a Sunday morning, but you can handle it!

Who knows what the women at the tomb in Matthew's story were thinking. They certainly didn't do any deep theology on the spot. The full realization of what they were confronted with would take many years to come about. For the moment, all they had was the tomb, the weirdness of the tomb's emptiness, the eerily absent Messiah, and the strange messenger from God who gave them a simple message that remains the core of the Good News:

> "He is not here! He has been raised! Go quickly! Tell his disciples, 'He has been raised from the dead, and he's going ahead of you to Galilee! You will see him there!'" (Matthew 28:6, my paraphrase.)

Once again, Matthew is a little different from the other Gospels. Consider Luke and John, where the disciples see Jesus a few times in and around Jerusalem soon after the resurrection. But this is Matthew. We'll let him tell the story his way.

Here is the Good News that Matthew proclaims: He is not here. He has been raised. Because he has been raised our world has changed in a profound and deep way. Now, go! Run! Tell his disciples! You will see him at home. Your home! Where you stay, where you live daily life, where you work, where you dwell, where your life has meaning on the most basic level. That is where you will see him!

When we let that sink in, we realize that the Good News of the empty tomb is not just something that we talk about at our church on a Sunday Morning. Talking about the Good News of the empty tomb at church is like talking about it in front of the empty tomb itself, and then leaving the conversation there, where no one else may hear it. But it is something that is meant to be carried forth from the tomb into everyday life, where we live, work, have our friendships and our relationships and our neighbors.

The Good News of God's new creation in Jesus, new life, a completely new start at truly human life the way God intends for it to be, is Good News that is meant to be taken into our everyday world and shared where it will transform our world.

For a congregation like ours, that means some things are going to change, as long as we are truly people of the empty tomb. It means new life for our faith community. That new life means nothing less than the recreation of our faith community in the name of the risen Lord Jesus.

To say the women at the tomb left quickly is an understatement. The text says they were *running*. As they ran, they went forth with a weird mix of feelings. The text says they felt fear. In this case that would be fear as in *sheer terror*. The Greek of Matthew's text uses the word *phobos*, which is *not* "awesome respect" (think of *phobia*, or better yet, think of the scariest thing in the scariest Stephen King movie or novel you've read). But the text also says they felt great (as in "mega-great") joy as they ran to tell the disciples the Good News that had been proclaimed to them.

And in their running they ran into Jesus, who very casually greeted them. They "worshiped" him, Matthew is very bad about filling in the details here, and then Jesus repeated the messenger's instructions. "Do not be afraid!" Again, this is afraid as in terrified, and, "go tell the others that I will see them at home, in Galilee." (Matthew 28:10, my paraphrase.)

On the side, I like the subtle message here from the Risen Lord himself that we should not do worship out of fear because someone has turned worship into law and expects us to do it and do it "properly," or else. Worship that invokes fear and is done out of fear is not worship but is a form of psychological abuse, toxic religion, and spiritual terrorism against the innocent.

But back on topic. The overall message, the Good News, is always the same:

Something has happened at the empty tomb and because of that the world has changed, from top to bottom, once and for all, forever! And this is Good News! The world is no longer the way it used to be. It has now been reset, at the empty tomb, with the powers of death and destruction put in their proper place.

Now the world is ready to begin again, resting on the edge of eternity with a vast future spread out before it. Now God moves forth from the empty tomb to work new creation in us, around us, and through us, regenerating us and our communities, recreating us, rebuilding our lives, and remaking our true selves in the image of God that we see in the risen Lord Jesus.

With this Good News in our hands we now go forth. We *run* with it into the world of our everyday lives. We allow it to transform us so that we may work to transform our faith community, our surrounding civil community, and our world.

This is where the cross has led us, to the tomb that stands empty, and before its entrance that stands open we find God's new creation staring us in the face, demanding our attention and our response as people of the resurrection.

Are we disturbed by that? Maybe. Maybe we lack confidence and maybe we lack vision. No one can see the future. But we have reassurance from Christ himself as we run forth into the world bearing the Good News:

"Do not be afraid!"

Now, go, and tell others that Christ has risen!

Peace be with you! Christ has risen!

ABOUT THE AUTHOR

Rev. Jack A. Wilder is a pastor in the Evangelical Lutheran Church in America. He has served congregations in upstate New York and east Tennessee since 1991. He is a graduate of Lutheran Theological Southern Seminary in Columbia, South Carolina, and is certified as an Intentional Interim Minister by the Center for Congregational Health. He also earned a Master of Arts degree in History from East Tennessee State University before becoming a pastor. He is currently the pastor of Gloria Dei Lutheran Church in Knoxville, Tennessee.

Jack A. Wilder

Made in the USA
Columbia, SC
07 April 2020